BIGGER
THAN
DATA

BIGGER THAN DATA

*A Law Enforcement Analyst's Roadmap
To Marketability, Professional Development,
Fulfillment & Joy*

Dawn Reeby

Editors: Million Dollar Story Agency
Book Design: Saqib Arshad
Cover Graphics: PixelStudio

Disclaimer

This book is for educational purposes only. The views expressed are those of the author alone. The reader is responsible for his or her own actions. Adherence to all applicable laws and regulations, including international, federal, state, and local governing professional licensing, business practices, advertising, and all other aspects of doing business in the United States, Canada, or any other jurisdiction, is the sole responsibility of the purchaser or reader. Neither the author nor the publisher assumes any responsibility or liability whatsoever on behalf of the purchaser or reader of these materials.

RISING GENIUSS TRANSFORMATION PROGRAM

Get the tools you need to become a TOP Law Enforcement Analyst and be incredibly SUCCESSFUL and HAPPY every step of the way! Analysts achieve a professional career that gives purpose, financial stability, and impact

IN UNISON with a personal life of balance and joy. Our RG Program is a one-stop shop for long-term, analytical success that lasts!

JOIN our FREE group & schedule a FREE CALL!

Join Our TRIBE OF EXCELLENCE!
https://www.facebook.com/groups/171925267401670

Book A FREE Call Today!
YES! WE CAN HELP YOU! Contact Us!
https://dawnreeby.podia.com/risinggeniussprogram

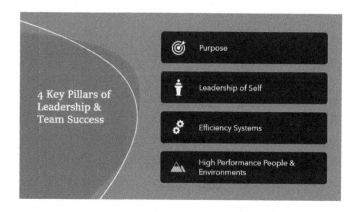

All solutions at Excellence in Analytics center around four success pillars:

Purpose, Leadership of Self, Efficiency Systems,

& High-Performance People and Environments

that, when seamlessly combined, produce impeccable and accelerated results!

This is my gift to you for buying this book
https://dawnreeby.podia.com/goal-crafting-achieving-in-le-analysis

This two-hour session walks you through
creating the right goals + developing intentional action steps to achieve them!

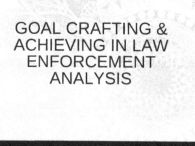

GOAL CRAFTING &
ACHIEVING IN LAW
ENFORCEMENT
ANALYSIS

Excellence in Analytics

ACKNOWLEDGMENTS

To my girls, Xiara and Ella. Always remember our mantra: "I am brave. I am strong. I am loved. I have courage, and I am humble and kind." Love you both with all my heart and soul.

Advance Praise/Endorsements

Dawn and I have worked together for many years, traveling the country as subject matter experts in crime analysis. In police agencies large and small, we have helped analysts and others to develop their knowledge, skills, and abilities and helped their agencies to build and expand analytical capacity. I have watched Dawn help analysts to really understand their data, improve their efficiency and build their confidence along the way. The end result is more actionable analysis that supports better policing and saves lives.

— Deb Piehl, Industry leader, SME, IADLEST Analytical Specialist, Private Consulting Business

As the Program Manager for the IADLEST TXDOT Data-Driven Approaches to Crime and Traffic Safety (DDACTS) program, I have had the pleasure of working with Dawn over the last six years on several different analytical related projects. During this time, I have watched as she has helped agencies and their analysts to create processes and procedures that allow the agency to follow best practices relating to law enforcement analysis. Dawn is an energetic analyst and trainer who has designed and delivered multiple nationally certified in-person, virtual, and hybrid analytical training workshops. She has worked with and provided technical assistance to analysts around the country, helping them to establish or grow their agency's analytical capacity. Dawn's unique delivery style and commitment to excellence shine through as she supports analysts and agencies at all levels. Her expertise is invaluable!"

— Daniel A. Howard, M.A., CPM, Retired Commander, Office of Professional Standards, IADLEST Texas- DDACTS Project Manager

As a military leader and public safety professional now leading my own team of intelligence analysts, I have experience in creating change in organizations and inspiring others to achieve beyond established norms. Dawn did an incredible job crafting what every analyst (and supervisor!) needs to know to build forward-leaning organizations capable of success through knowledge and a positive attitude. As a leader in this profession for many years, I personally look for the qualities, mindset, and characteristics described by Dawn in all my analysts and leaders. Now is the time to make awesome happen in yourself and in your organization. I highly recommend that all levels of analytical professionals digest this book multiple times and fully embrace the work-life integration model proposed throughout this masterpiece!"

— Colonel Alvin Schwapp, Military leader, CT State Police Intelligence Leader

As Vice President of Administration of the IACA, subject matter expert in analytics for over 42 years, author of multiple law enforcement analytical presentations, and partner in crime with Dawn throughout many coaching deliveries, I fully see the value in this much-needed book! Dawn's unique approach to building effective analytical systems in alignment with *leadership of self* unveils what is truly missing from this industry. Analysts who follow this guide fully will gain the mindset and tools needed to create a long-term, valued career in law enforcement analytics!

— Annie Mitchell, Industry leader, Subject Matter Expert, Vice President of Admin for IACA, private consulting business

As a Chief of Police, national data-driven strategies instructor, and wellness advocate, I deeply support and respect the work that Dawn does to lead police analysts, supervisors, and leaders into holistic success. She is an industry leader in analytics and in wellness and is a catalyst of positive change! This book holds key concepts that will shift the culture in law enforcement to produce excellence in analytics in unison with excellence in personal life.

— Chief Christopher Chew, Chief of Evesham, NJ Police

As a Board member of the California Crime and Intelligence Analyst Association and long-time crime analyst, I have personally been inspired by Dawn and the work of Excellence in Analytics. Dawn is an influencer in the law enforcement analytical community, and her presentations on creating value and buy-in truly help analysts move their agencies from inefficient and reactive into efficient, proactive, data-driven machines that deliver excellence with purpose, confidence, and drive. Every analyst in the world must read this book as it truly uncovers the totality of skills and character needed to excel in this industry.

— Dana Boss, Past President of the Central Valley Crime and Intelligence Analysts Association, Board Member of California Crime and Intelligence Analysts Association, Cold Case Foundation Analyst, and Crime Analyst for Reedley Police Department

Dawn's commitment to inspiring and leading others into their own wellness is transformational! I echo the sentiments of the IACA with their confidence in awarding her the 2021 Bryan Hill Memorial Award for her contribution to the professional success of other analysts by sharing her knowledge, her examples, and her time freely and selflessly. As a supporter of the law enforcement analytical community myself, I'm particularly excited to see this book address the specific wellness needs of the civilians and sworn who commit their lives to quality analytics in policing. I congratulate her not only for her success but for her continuous contributions to the success of others!

— Manny San Pedro, Crime Analysis Podcast (Canada)

Dawn and I have partnered on multiple wellness initiatives over the last nine years, and her insight and enthusiasm in seeing others succeed in creating their lives by design are astounding! Her commitment to inspiring and leading others into their own transformational wellness has been phenomenal to watch unfold. As a family with a lineage in policing, I'm particularly excited to see this book address the specific wellness needs of the civilian and sworn heroes of the law enforcement community. Bravo to this incredibly valuable tool that supports a culture shift in the emergency response industry and beyond. It's needed now more than ever!

— Matthew and Jamie MacKenzie, Matthew Founder of
River Rock Excursions and Jamie MacKenzie,
Transformative wellness and Business Coach
riverrockexcursions.com, jamiemackenziewellness.com

CONTENTS

PREFACE

The world we live in runs on data. That means the world is, in some ways, run by data analysts. Don't believe me? Here are a few industries that rely heavily on interpretations from analysts:

- Sports
- Banking and Investment
- Education
- Communications
- Government and Public Sector

And that's just a partial list. It should come as no surprise that Law Enforcement relies on data analysts. Law Enforcement Analysts are responsible for researching, assembling, analyzing, evaluating, and reporting intelligence information and crime data so that agencies can use information to drive effective and efficient strategies. It sounds like a pretty big job, right?

If you're a Law Enforcement Analyst, you may have laughed at that question. Of course, it is enormous. You also know that it's not easy, and it's a job that faces a wide array of challenges.

PURPOSE

Analysts and supervisors in law enforcement undoubtedly give much of themselves in service. However, they often lack the organizational structure, resources, and efficiencies that traditional industries take for granted. They regularly find themselves operating with fragmented systems at work and spending late nights, lunches, and weekends catching up. Analysts make a habit of taking on way more than they can handle. They give so much of themselves to their careers that they have little left in the engine at the end of the day, leading to high divorce rates, increased illness, poor personal wellness, and a *significant lack of self-care!*

Because they honor their roles and responsibilities with pride and deep conviction, they work harder – not smarter – and continue the cycle of inefficiency and burnout. With such high career demands, they sacrifice their personal goals, health, finances, and relationships with families and friends. As such, they cannot achieve their best lives. They struggle to elevate, inspire, and empower themselves into living lives that are full of joy and fulfillment. They are overwhelmed and searching for calmness in the storm.

I've had the honor to work with hundreds of analysts in the US through coaching and in-person and online training. I was also an analyst at multiple police agencies for many years starting in the late 1990s. I find that analysts and supervisors face the same challenges, including feeling undervalued, not having a definite direction, and lacking time management and productivity. Many of these deserving professionals feel burnt out and simply don't take care of themselves. Two-hundred-forty US Law

Enforcement Analysts responded to a 2019 National Highway Traffic Safety Administration (NHTSA) survey indicating time management was a top challenge – they suffered from work overload, competing priorities, and not enough time. So, they brought work home with them regularly or skipped breaks and lunches... and eventually got *very burnt out!*

Not only do I coach and train analysts and supervisors out of this negative cycle, but I also run a Facebook group that supports Law Enforcement Analysts and supervisors called <u>TRIBE OF EXCELLENCE</u> (<u>https://bit.ly/2WptDCf</u>.)

In 2020, 70% of respondents to the group's entry survey reported *finding more time* and *being burnt out* were their biggest challenges. With the considerable changes to our work environments due to COVID, we are even more vulnerable to the habits that perpetuate this situation and our overwhelm.

These professionals are not alone. And if this sounds like you, you are not alone! I know what it is like to wear a mask, suffer from adrenal fatigue, put all my energy into work, and miss out on the beautiful life, relationships, and adventure right in front of me. I know what it is like to push my limits, thinking I would reap the benefits at a later time that never seemed to come. I know what it's like to hide the truth behind a suit and continuously have my health and wellness take a back seat to work.

I remember when I couldn't answer the question, "What are twenty things you like to do?" I was a mom, the breadwinner, an analyst, and an instructor. Besides some obligations to family and friends, there wasn't much more to me that I nurtured. I loved myself, mostly.... I just didn't *know* myself. So, when a friend asked me the twenty things I liked to do, I was embarrassed to only come up with a handful. I had not established clear boundaries with family, friends, or work.

I served others most of the time and was not creating my best life by design. I had no idea who I was outside of the walls of work and parenthood. I was reactive, suppressed by guilt and the desire to be of value, and my lack of quality and joyous life outside of work was proof of my culpability. I did not lead my life. My life led me. Until I decided to change - and now I show others at an agency, department, and individual level how to change, too. In fact...

This book is all about *transforming* you into a *proactive, professional genius* who is *productive, innovative, confident, efficient, growth-oriented, and a deeply valued professional leader* who *thrives* due to work/life harmony. My goal is to equip you with the tools you need to create maximum efficiencies and proactive police strategies in connection with the leadership of your professional and personal self. Be prepared to engage with the process and learn action steps you can implement today!

The following chapters map seven modules in the *Rising Genius Transformation Program (RG)* which is a complete, comprehensive step-by-step roadmap for success habits and *excellence in analytics.* This book will help you begin your journey in excellence. The book plus the course will transform your trajectory, personally and professionally, because the system delivers the following for you or you and your team:

1. EXCELLENT career paths that align with purpose, passion, and skillset.

2. EXCELLENT, efficient, and maximized processes.
3. EXCELLENT analyst wellness and leadership of self.
4. EXCELLENT leadership of industry and others.
5. EXCELLENT recruitment, retention, and support of Law Enforcement Analysts.

INTRODUCTION

Are you ready to skyrocket your results, multiply your productivity, and get connected with other high-level, service-based thinkers from around the world?

Hi, I'm Dawn Reeby, Founder and CEO of Excellence in Analytics (EIA.) My mission is to ignite your desire for excellence in your professional and personal life and empower your pursuit of that excellence.

I've enjoyed working with hundreds of analysts worldwide as a subject matter expert, best practices designer, and instructor for IADLEST, IACA, NHTSA, IACP, TXDOT, and other federal think tanks. Through these contracts, I've flown around the country building analytical capacity in agencies. I've designed and instructed in-person and virtual strategy and technical training. I ran the first mastermind solely for Law Enforcement Analysts and created the first analyst library. I've also been a Keynote speaker at many law enforcement and analyst-centric conferences.

Out of all these experiences, my heart is happiest and most fulfilled working one-on-one with analysts and supervisors to build their confidence and skills, develop roadmaps for their success, and let them know they are *bigger than data*; as human beings, they have value and a right to finding joy in their lives and work. I strive to help them attain work-life integration that brings excellence to all areas of their lives because I believe we deserve more. As a law enforcement analytical subject matter expert, I'm here to help you create your roadmap to marketability, professional development, fulfillment, and joy!

The premise of this book is to ...

- Provide new and aspiring Law Enforcement Analysts the mindset and tools needed to become the best version of themselves, personally and professionally.
- Provide new solutions for proactive, data-driven strategies in the most impactful and sustainable way.
- Increase efficiencies and save resources of time, money, and energy.
- Shift the culture in law enforcement to produce excellence in analytics in unison with excellence in personal life.

Work Smarter, Not Harder

You've heard it before - we all strive to work smarter, not harder. We, in policing, are typically reactive. A crime occurs, someone calls the police, the police arrive on-scene and diffuse, arrest, have a shootout, whatever. But what if, instead, we could use data-driven strategies to limit reactive scenarios? This concept of being proactive versus reactive has grown into a new way of policing and a new way of living. As a result, leaders develop the desire and strategies to succeed in their analytical and personal lives. These individuals have a more significant impact on law enforcement, grow a solid foundation in analytics, and maintain excellent personal balance. They build skills and confidence to truly excel.

Keep reading if you, as a Law Enforcement Analyst, or a Law Enforcement Department Head, are ready to achieve the following:

- Grow confidence. Feel empowered. Become proud of your quality work.
- Grow a solid foundation in your career faster and with focused resources.
- Create work/life harmony.
- Have a more significant impact.
- Maximize resources and create efficiencies.
- Create excellent personal leadership and balance.
- Establish an unwavering belief in yourself.
- Reach goals faster and with much more confidence and ease.
- Transform your quality of life and work by becoming highly effective, productive, and joyous.
- Become super confident in your career.
- Be an industry leader, get the job you want, get paid well, and feel valued.
- Work smarter, not harder.

In Summary...

Yes! You can have it all. Catapult your career while creating work-life harmony with *leadership of self* as your top priority. As a result of thriving in the *transformation training* and *clarity coaching* that you will find in this book and in the programs we also offer, you will develop the desire and strategies to achieve success in your work and personal life. You will create a more significant impact in your career and maintain excellent personal balance. You will learn tips and tricks to become highly effective and productive in less time and with less energy. You will learn to work smarter, not harder while increasing your productivity tenfold. This step-by-step *transformation training* will help you assess key growth areas in the law enforcement analytical field and personal leadership, create a comprehensive development plan, and launch yourself to success!

MODULE 1

GAIN CLARITY AND ALIGNMENT WITH YOUR DESIRED REALITY, PURPOSE, SKILLS, AND TALENTS

> *"Within a short time of crystalizing my vision through coaching and the growth work, it all started to come true!"*
>
> - ANDREW BUTTS

Why This Matters

I want to share what I learned from a fascinating book, *The 5 Regrets of the Dying,* by Bronnie Ware. She spent her career sitting by the bedsides of dying people and noticed a common theme of what they wished they hadn't done. The number one regret of people on their deathbed was that they wished they hadn't worked so much. The second regret of people facing the end of their lives - that particularly relates to our lesson on *why* - was that they wished that they had lived a life true to themselves.

Instead of living for everyone else's expectations, they wished they had lived a life that was true to *their* 'why,' skills, talents, and things that lit them up inside! Why do we work so hard, putting income creation ahead of all other decisions in our lives?

Money and stuff don't create happiness.

Happiness raises your vibration and brings about money and stuff!

I, too, had to spend time getting crystal clear on what I wanted in my own life. I had to stop and think about what I wanted in my family relationships, friendships and social circles, physical body, philanthropic efforts, and other vital areas of my life. When I created clarity around these essential areas, decisions regarding where I spent my time, energy, and money became more manageable and more intentional and focused. And funny enough, my work productivity increased as well.

Let me share an example. I took a six-figure contract because the work was interesting, and the money was fabulous. But I soon realized that the role didn't align with my core values and vision for my life. I spent three-plus hours a day commuting, had to get my workouts in at 4 am if I could, spent zero time with my family, and was always exhausted.

I made the hard decision to leave but leaving opened a new opportunity for me, a gift. Now I use my skills and talents, creating, with ease and flow, a legacy business that supports analysts throughout the world! I help inspire analysts to want more, find their genius, and empower them to achieve exactly what they want. I am energized and fulfilled in my career. I exercise daily, have breakfast with my daughter every morning, and pick her up right after school. We spend a ton of quality time together! I live my *life by design*, and you can, too!

I will help point you in the direction you belong or strengthen the path you have determined to be your purpose. Begin to think about who you are and who your most authentic self is today.

Defining Your Purpose:

How to Achieve Alignment With Your Purpose Necessary To Gain Focus And Direction

Module 1 (in both this book and my course) helps create clarity around your desired reality, purpose, and skillset, which are *key* to creating the compass for your Professional Development Blueprint. Here is where you define your dream about what you want to be true, what you want your life to be. What drives you to do more, be more, serve more. You define that life by design fueled by purpose and talent, and let it drive you to excel! You discover and use your skills and talents to become the best possible you. In this stage, you determine what's most important in your life and how you can best serve others with your talents while creating balance and harmony in your personal life.

Your Best Outcome

There is a better way. Just like we tell our officers to be proactive, we can create more innovative processes that enable us to see the open doors and fly free! Imagine feeling:

- Valued
- Confident
- Knowledgeable
- Purposeful
- On the right career path
- Balanced
- Proactive
- Strong in your vision of your analytical goals
- Cared for deeply
- In the flow
- At ease
- An essential part of the team
- Joyous at home
- Fully trained

When we shift our mindsets and create effective habits and strategies in our own lives, we create *simple excellence* that best serves our police departments *and* ourselves. This book and the related course are all about implementing research-based methodologies that will ensure your success. You will become more valued, more confident, more knowledgeable, more purposeful, more proactive, and more in harmony with a life you love to live. The way you design your life – both at work and home – is precisely how it will be. Yes, *you* have the power to shift your life into whatever you want it to be. I'm going to show you how. I invite you to be a participating partner on this journey of finding your harmony!

Smart Strategy

Life By Design. Your Desired Reality.

Defining your *desired reality* is vital in everything you do from this point forward. We can start to make choices today to find our true selves and live our lives with design, purpose, and impact. So, if you're sitting at a desk for nine hours straight or if you haven't gone to the gym in months even though you promised yourself you would, it's because *you* design your life this way. On the other hand, if you have blossoming relationships with family and friends and you find ease and happiness in the work you do, it's because, again, *you* designed your life this way. At this point, you don't have to know the *how*. That will come. Instead, you will grow into alignment by creating a focus on *what* you want - and that growth is essential! We can start to make choices today to find our true selves and live our lives with purpose and impact, and truly by design.

Defining your desired reality is the first step so, let's get to it. What is the reality that you desire? What do you want your life to look like? What do you want your family relationships to feel like? Your friendships to be like? What does playtime look like for you? Traveling the world? Quiet time alone in nature? Curled up with a great book? What are your physical body goals? Your health goals? What are your philanthropic interests that light you up? How much money do you want to make? What does your investment and legacy look like? What does your home look and feel like? What does your best career look like?

Below is a bubble chart that I use as a teaching aid in my course. One thing you'll notice is that the chart doesn't just say career. We, as analysts, often get so ultra-focused on our professional lives that we neglect other essential parts of our existence that require equal effort and attention. This tool can help you explore all areas of your life that you want to design – because there is so much more to you than work!

EXCELLENCE IN ANALYTICS

I want you to have your best career ever in harmony with doing the things you love with the people you adore for reasons that are meaningful to you. I want this for you today. Not tomorrow, not a month or year from now, but today. You may not know it now, or perhaps you do, but you deserve to live an abundant and joyous life. Find your excellence in career and in life alongside people who will elevate you. You deserve greatness. You deserve to live a life filled with laughs, unraveling, memories, and dancing legs! You deserve to find your inner genius!

Your Purpose. Your why.

Now, let's take some time to explore creating clarity around your 'why,' defining your skills and talents, and then bringing you to action in your own life! Knowing your why is at the core of it all. That is where we gain clarity on our purpose and dream about what we want to be true, what we want our lives and contributions to be. What drives us to do more, be more, serve more. We define that purpose and let it cause us to excel! We discover and use our skills and talents to become our best possible selves. In this stage, we determine what drives our efforts and how we can best serve others with our talents while creating balance and harmony in our personal lives.

Why start with *why*? Great leaders inspire action by creating a core connection to the bigger picture. What's your purpose? What's your cause? What's your belief? In his book "*Start with Why*," Simon Sinek shares that the most outstanding leaders in their industry – those at Apple, Southwest Air, Harley Davidson, and others – focus on *why* they do what they do, not *what* or *how* they do it. His best-selling book and famous TED Talk illustrate that we should start with complete clarity of our why. The discipline of *what* and the consistency of *how* will come. He explains this concept using Apple Computers as an example. He shares that if the company were like other companies, their marketing strategy would say, "We make great computers. They're beautifully designed, simple to use, and user-friendly. Want to buy one?" Meh. If Apple were to market and communicate like this, with the *'what'* (make computers), they probably wouldn't be so successful. Here's how Apple conveys what they believe; "Everything we do, we believe in challenging the status quo. We believe in thinking differently. We challenge the status quo by making our products beautifully designed, simple to use, and user-friendly. We just happen to make great computers. Want to buy one?" Different, right?

Many authors, research, and transformational speakers start with 'why.' Martin Luther King, Jr. started with a strong 'why,' which was his dream of bringing equality to America. He didn't focus on the 'how.' He didn't say, "The way I'm going to do this is XXX." He focused on his dream first. He gave his speech eight times; "I have a dream!" He created purpose and intention, and those drove all his actions.

Now it's time to clarify your *why* and your skills and talents. Be crystal clear about what you want from all facets of your life, and why you are willing to deliver excellence to achieve them. Determine how much energy you choose to give and own those decisions. Start with what gives you joy! Do you regularly jump into your workday with a commitment to accomplishing an explicit goal? Are you driven to solve cases, provide more than the basic intelligence, going beyond the first keystroke, because you are deeply connected to the case outcome? Are you willing to dive deeper to serve victims of domestic violence because you know someone who suffered? Do you feel energized and inspired to bring value and drive even more remarkable achievements in forensics, human or animal trafficking cases, crash reduction because perhaps these issues are deep in your core? Think about the life you want to live six months from now, one year from now, five years from now, the value you want to contribute. Dream it, and the Universe will make it appear. Envision your greater purpose and become aligned with that purpose.

You might be thinking right now, "I don't have a big *why*. I'm lucky to survive the day without getting fired. I've never figured out my 'why' between running around at work and shuffling the kids between sports. I'm stuck. I just kind of fell into this all. Maybe when I was a college student, I had some big dreams, but now I have a real life. I don't have a compass pointing me in any direction. I feel like I'm aimlessly floating. Like what I do and don't do depends on what others in my environment decide is best. I'm working for my paycheck/retirement/health benefits." Do you want to know something? There is a better way. You don't have to keep floating and wondering.

Recognizing And Growing Your Unique Skills

We also want to consider our unique skills and talents *long before* we are on our deathbeds. We are inherently incredible at crucial skills. For instance, numbers make sense to me. Do they make much sense to you? I have a budget, by month, for the last 10+ years of all my home expenses by line item. I list my mortgage, utilities, groceries, school tuition, etc., in the top half of the spreadsheet. Then I list my income projections and actuals and can tell you how much money I'm predicting I will save by month for the entire year. Tracking my numbers gives me clarity, a feeling of control, and a financial compass. I have friends who would pull their hair out if they even dreamt about documenting their budget items in a spreadsheet. They can't even stomach the *word* 'spreadsheet,' never mind consistently and accurately tabulate said activities. These are *my* talents and abilities. My friends certainly have their valuable talents and skills as well.

Defining our purpose within the context of our skills and talents will accelerate our progress towards our goals. What are the skills and talents that you like about yourself the most? When are you the proudest? The most confident? Once you identify what core skills and talents you bring to the table, you must continue to nourish them with training, growth opportunities, and utilization at the right agency.

Now you understand that crafting your *why* establishes the direction to where you will point your compass and is indeed the starting point for professional and personal mastery.

Success Highlights

Rhea G. was an analyst at an agency undergoing extraordinary change with three different chiefs and other transitioning leadership personnel. She lost her cheerleaders and found herself in an incredibly stressful work environment where many were jumping ship. She felt like she was on a ledge, ready to crash. As Kismet had it, one morning while scrolling LinkedIn, she saw an RG ad that read, "Do you want to find your genius?" and immediately leaped. Rhea regularly invested in her personal growth and knew she needed to dive into something big. Through the tears, the growth work, and the deep stares in the mirror, Rhea found herself again. She found her confidence, her path, her energy, her solution. Rhea smiled again. With her coach in her corner, she found a new job that better aligned with her skills and direction, released her imposter syndrome, and found a happier life by design. We are incredibly proud of Rhea and the commitment she has as a leader in the industry! She has graduated from our Rising GENIUSS Transformation Program (RG) and is now one of our beloved coaches, guiding others into their authority, authenticity, and influence in their lives.

Inspired Action Exercise

I hope it has become crystal clear to you how important it is to start with our desired reality, *why*, and organic skillset. Those who do so find joy, focus, and value in the work they do. Proactively designing the lives we dream of living and focusing on our 'why' gives us the direction or the compass for our life. Decisions, training, growth work.... These will all grow out of our 'why.' Creating clarity will give you the direction just like it gave me, the leaders studied by Simon Sinek, Martin Luther King, Jr., and many others who have gone on to be incredible leaders with impeccable value and balance. Linking your purpose with the skills and talents that inherently come to you will create direction, purpose, and a deep sense of satisfaction and value.

Below are a series of questions for you to explore deeply so that you may grow. These directional questions will help you begin to think about who you are and who your most genuine self is. They will start to point you in the direction you belong or strengthen the direction you have determined is your purpose. Once you have a focus/a compass, you will be able to design your advancements and efforts more easily in other areas of your work and life. Explore these questions with openness and honesty. Here we go.

1. What do you want? What do you want in your life? When you stop and think about this, it might be hard to articulate. What do you want without considering anyone else?

2. Where do you want to be in one year? Three years? Five years? If you don't know where you're going, you'll never get there. Where do you want to be? Look up from the daily chaos and explore where you want to be. Who do you want to become?

3. What lights you up? What inspires you? What gives you energy? What gives you joy? What makes you come alive?

4. What skills and talents do you like about yourself the most? When are you the proudest? Most confident? List as many as you can. Then list more!

5. What's your *why*? What drives you to succeed? What drives you to push through discomfort and accelerate?

6. What is your non-negotiable? What *must* you have in your life by design?

My gift to you: Life by Design

> *I am struggling with work-life harmony. How do I begin to create my Life by Design?*

The first step is to *decide.* Decide what you want your life to look like. Use this free Life by Design (http://bitly.ws/gMw8) download to gain clarity on your purpose and desired lifestyle. This is the roadmap to becoming a purpose-driven analytical professional who delivers impact while maintaining your well-being.

MODULE 2

ELEVATE YOUR SKILLS AND COMPETENCIES

> *"Dawn possesses the rare talent and ability to be a master at all types of data analysis while also being able to coach and teach anyone in an easy-to-understand way regardless of their level of experience."*
> — CHIEF LANCE ARNOLD

Why This Matters

The purpose of Module 2 is to help you create clarity around your current technology and analytical competencies, to identify and close any gaps between your existing talents and abilities, and to develop your long-term strategic analyst strategy. Doing so will give you the confidence and roadmap to career success. Before we begin, it's essential to understand why sharpening your skills is necessary. Let me share a story with you.

I remember a day at a police agency; I came across a case involving a three-year-old girl, "Baby Brielle." Warning - the following few paragraphs are graphic, so if you are reading this but are not in law enforcement, you may want to skip forward.

I had left a *very* challenging relationship two and a half years before seeing this case, taking my then fifteen- and one-year-old daughters with me. "Baby Brielle" - who was around the same age as my sweet, cuddly, younger daughter - was beaten by her twenty-five-year-old mother of five. The mother beat her daughter *to death* because she was angry that the girl had wet herself and that Brielle had gone into the kitchen at night searching for food.

According to the newspaper, the autopsy revealed over 50 injuries to the child: various bruises found head to toe; multiple contusions found on her ears and face; broken ribs and bruised lungs; and a subdural hematoma in her head eventually led to Brielle's death. The mother attacked the child twice during the incident, throwing her into furniture and across the room and banging her head against the floor. The mother assaulted her three-year-old with such force that she injured her own toe and hand. The boyfriend had witnessed the abuse but had gone back to sleep during the attack.

Looking at her autopsy photos was heart-breaking. Her tiny, lifeless, blueish body was the same size as my daughter's vibrant one. Her limp hands were so *small,* and the image of her purpled skin and lips burned a hole in my brain and heart. I went home that day and hugged my warm daughter, feeling her tiny fingers in my hands and covering her pink cheeks with more kisses than ever – if that's even possible. I looked into her innocent eyes and felt the pain that the little girl must have felt each day, knowing that she was never cared for in the same, loving, nurturing way.

It was then that I gained *my why*. I wanted to *do* something. I wanted to *be impactful*. I wanted to *use* my skills and talents to find the right suspect in this case and in all similar cases that would cross my path. I was thankful for the skills I had learned during my career to date and the habits I put into place. I was grateful for all the databases I knew thoroughly. I appreciated my keen attention to detail which gave me the power to do something! I was thankful I had sharpened my analytical saw; I continued the connections and analytics that would bring justice to those little hands and feet lying on that cold, silver table... those little hands and feet that would never feel the earth beneath her toes again.

I realized I have a gift and *must sharpen* this gift *every day* for all those families who would need my skills to be *excellent* at the moment of their crisis. I vowed to serve them most effectively – to the best of my capabilities. I did so for Baby Brielle, others like her, and for my family, who had risen from domestic abuse. And *that* was my *why*. That, paired with my skills and talents, is what kept me focused and service-minded. My *why* was what I returned to when my career compass spiraled.

You have the gift, too! *You* are assigned to analysis, and *you* have the *opportunity* to use your gifts for others. *Your* journey - of building your analytical skills so that *you* can be *impactful* - starts today. You can help keep families and officers *safe* with your habits and practices.

Together, we can find a voice for all the Baby Brielle's in this world and work to *prevent* such travesty. Together we can create *impact* by sharpening our skills and *believing* we are part of something *much, much bigger!*

Your Best Outcome

Be strategic about continuous growth; establish a development roadmap. You know your *why* now, and you know you want to build your analytical skills so that what you do has impact. Be strategic with how you go about adding and honing your skills; start by creating a development roadmap for yourself and your career path.

Many analysts receive little to no training even though they must keep up with the ever-changing tools and tactics to produce quality results. Analysts must analyze data every day and produce actionable reports, staying proactive, busy with purpose, and connected to resources. Part of developing professionally must include building partnerships and creating systems and processes. But to do that effectively and efficiently, it is imperative for both the analyst and the department to prioritize outcomes, create a vision supporting those outcomes, and have a blueprint in place to get there.

Typically, agencies do not have the proper budget in place for training that supports their analyst's growth. Meanwhile, analysts may not yet have the experience to select results-focused courses and training sessions that will advance their skills effectively and purposefully.

Rather than following an intentional, continuous education roadmap that supports an overall vision, an analyst often selects training that is opportunistic. In other words, their decision is based on whatever floats by their desk or comes to their attention through the office or department grapevine. As such, analysts attend training sessions sporadically when they can fit them in.

Not having a developmental roadmap isn't the only thing that can sabotage an analyst's effort towards skill improvement. Often after these fragmented training sessions, analysts return to a demanding environment and a backlog of work that piled up while they were away for training; at best, they incorporate only small portions of what they learned. A month, or even a week after training, most of the material they received remains buried in books, now collecting dust in their filing cabinets.

Hopefully, you appreciate the necessity to establish, prioritize, and then regularly revisit a professional development roadmap based on desired results relative to the analyst's vision, skills, talents, and passions. Ideally, a professional development roadmap should include relevant training based on selected skills, quality networking, instructional efforts, building buy-in, leadership development, and other results-focused growth opportunities.

By providing this type of professional development, agencies will experience a higher quality of analyses driven by motivated and inspired analysts, agency buy-in, improved data quality systems, lower frequencies of crashes, crimes and social harms, higher clearance rates, and so much more. Both the agency and the analyst benefit from actionable information consistently when they partner to build an intentional, effective, reproducible system for creating and evaluating effective strategies based on proactive analysis. Essentially, agencies must be outcome-oriented when developing a roadmap to fill gaps, encourage learning, and promote ownership and growth in their analysts.

Smart Strategy

This module focuses on essential steps to take to be excellent in analytics. First, design a strategic professional roadmap. If you are unsure of how best to do this, get help.

As you will discover in this chapter, there are many different types of analysis that require unique skills. Some will focus more on statistics whereas others will focus more on linking people and places. All of them require critical thinking, curiosity, and data accessibility and querying. Our coaching programs have assessments and training tools for each type of analysis which allow analysts to fast track their success on their career path. They get aligned with their specific track and avoid falling into the trap of 'shiny object training'.

Professional development moves you away from isolation and reactivity by walking you through the technology and analytical skills needed for efficiency, proficiency, and success in law enforcement analysis. If you aspire to *excellence* in your work, you need to sharpen your saw; i.e., develop your skills. In this case, the skills we are talking about include database management, trend analysis, pattern identification, computer applications, automation efforts, actionable reporting, critical thinking, etc. Making a difference as a Law Enforcement Analyst starts with reading reports daily, using thresholds to identify patterns and trends, and being curious. Quality data must exist to develop strategic operations using data-driven efforts. My goal is to create clarity for you around current technology and analytical skills status and help set up goals and timelines to develop your professional development roadmap.

We will spend time exploring specific skills in data integration, data quality, technology and products, and types of law enforcement analysis. These categories and skillsets are derived from the International Association of Crime Analysts (IACA) Certification skills, assessments that I have performed with numerous analysts country-wide, and from 23+ years in law enforcement, along with skills I personally find to be most helpful. Exploring this material will help you determine if you're exceeding your department's expectations and provide insight into potential opportunities for your advancement.

First comes analysis. After all, we are analysts. It's essential to recognize which analysis type to utilize; they include tactical, strategic, administrative, operational, and intelligence analysis. Each is outlined briefly on the following pages and the related skills are often unique to that specific role. Note that some analysts must perform many of the types of analysis below but it's important to understand that you shouldn't necessarily be an expert at all of them. Instead, work with your agency to decide the *primary* impact goal of your analytical role.

Tactical Analysis

Tactical analysis is the study of short-term series or patterns that typically help with patrol deployment strategies and suspect or lead identification. The types of skills needed for tactical analysis include gaining access to police records management systems and open data sources, connecting the dots between these multiple sources, identifying and finalizing patterns and series as they emerge, utilizing best practice techniques to analyze these patterns for location, time, victim, offender, and modus operandi, performing temporal and spatial analyses, performing predictions on next hit locations, creating impact products that effectively disseminate information to the police, and relaying suggested tactics for offender apprehension, suppression, and opportunity-blocking. Technologies used often in tactical analysis include Microsoft Access and Excel and mapping programs. Note that technologies are regularly changing, which is why we won't list too many tools here as they may become obsolete. But our team continuously updates training tools in our programs so that analysts are as up to date as possible in their skills development.

Strategic Analysis

Strategic analysis studies long-term statistical trends, hot spots, and problems, develops strategies to address identified problems, and uses evaluation tools to assess process and impact of related strategies. This can include crash, crime, and social harm trends. This type of analyst identifies a problem (such as copper theft from vacant buildings, increased motor vehicle thefts, prostitution, and tire/rim thefts) or a problem location (such as a hotel/motel). That specific analysis is then used to develop strategies to respond to the problem. The types of skills needed for strategic analysis include identifying trends of day of week, correlation, time of day, repeat offenders, repeat victims, threshold analysis, and similar, and are often conducted in Microsoft Access and Excel. Analysts use calculations such as frequencies, percent change, and cross-tabulations to measure the progress of the problems as well as evaluate the success and gaps in any strategies implemented. Analysts also provide key recommendations relative to suggested strategies and must be current on national best practices. The Center for Problem-Oriented Policing is a terrific resource for analysts performing strategic analysis.

Administrative Analysis

Administrative analysis involves producing statistical reports, research, and other long-term projects. Analysts performing administrative analysis typically produce statistical reporting such as Uniform Crime Report (UCR) or Incident-Based Reporting System (IBRS) reports, charts and graphs to support the chief's presentation to the City Council, crime/crash statistics to support grant applications, and similar. Like strategic analysis, administrative analysis involves utilizing a lot of functions and formulas in Microsoft Excel or Access, creating graphs and charts, and using visual aid programs (such as Power BI, Tableau, mapping software, and similar) to relay the analysis.

Operational Analysis

Operational analysis is analysis relative to the department's operations and includes districting or redistricting analysis, patrol staffing analysis, cost-benefit analysis, and special event resource deployment. The technical skills required here mirror strategic and administrative analysis. Analysts performing this type of analysis may also need to understand budgeting, geography, and City initiatives.

Intelligence Analysis

Intelligence analysis studies the relationships between criminal enterprises such as gangs, human trafficking networks, drug cartels, organized retail criminal networks, and similar. This type of analysis encompasses repeat offender/victim analysis, commodity flow analysis, social media analysis, and communication analysis. An intelligence analyst knows how to perform cell phone studies, person/network connections, and visual charting. They understand social networking analysis, can create timelines to represent connected series of events and people, track and collate intelligence information from field interviews, surveillance, investigations, arrests, prosecutions, and from other agencies, identify threats facing the community, the state, and the nation, and use their technology skills to link people, locations, and patterns. These analysts use Microsoft Access, link charting tools, and have a thorough understanding of social media and the intelligence cycle.

Regardless of which type of analysis you are performing (tactical, strategic, administrative, operational, or intelligence), your number one goal is *to provide actionable reporting so that your officers, command staff, and detectives can succeed.* You must create products and services that provide *impact.* That means that you are regularly identifying patterns and trends, identifying potential suspect leads, answering the question "Why", and contributing in an essential way to your agency's operations. You will need key technology, analytical, and other skills to achieve the desired impact.

Here are key activities and skills that every analyst must obtain and nurture regularly, albeit that their overall functions might differ based on role responsibilities.

Create Quality Systems

Invest the time developing systems that allow data to be at your fingertips. This means do everything you can to get access to your records management and dispatch systems in a way that is usable and easily accessible. Far too many analysts spend so much of their time extracting and cleaning data that they don't have time for the analysis of it. This is a critical mistake. Develop the systems needed to have all your data stored in one spot, easily accessible, easily searchable, and easily reportable. Then spend the time getting to know your data inside and out. This may mean that you must perform data integrations, develop master files where years of data relative to your study area (crash, crime, drugs, etc.) are in one easy location, and establish systematic processes to improve data quality.

Data quality must be a priority for an agency that truly desires to implement data-driven strategies. Although analysts are in the data on a regular basis, they should not be considered the primary data quality agents of an agency's efforts. Instead, the analyst can identify data quality challenges that must be addressed on a systems level. The most long-term and time-efficient efforts involve creating systems of success at multiple levels within the agency. Click Data Quality Tips for Analysts https://bit.ly/3kRolZy for a free download on how to get started with implementing systemic data quality improvements.

Finally, analysts will want to spend time developing automated reporting systems using tools such as Microsoft Access, SSRS, or some other system that easily extracts, reports, and creates space to analyze the data. Overall, having access to quality data will give you the tools needed to succeed as it did for me in the Baby Brielle case and throughout my analytical career.

Analyze Data Daily

As noted earlier, your number one goal is *to provide actionable reporting so that your officers, command staff and detectives can succeed.* This means that you are reading reports daily (larger agencies may have to systematize this process), performing threshold analyses to automatically identify data fluctuations, digging into those data fluctuations using the comprehensive systems you created to identify why they exist, and simply getting curious about your data. Think critically about what your data is telling you, and not telling you. Be innovative and find information that may not exist in your current data set (i.e., pawn data, probation/parole data, Department of Motor Vehicle information, etc.). To achieve this, you must regularly establish data querying tools that keep you confident with your analysis and give you the accessibility to dig deeper and answer the question "Why?".

Produce Actionable Reports

Statistics are not enough. I repeat... *statistics are not enough!* Every product that leaves your hands must be actionable. An officer should be able to read your one-page report and know exactly where to spend most of his/her time during that shift. Avoid the trap of regurgitating information. No one needs a list of reports that they wrote. Instead, they need to understand the relationships between those reports and others that only analysts have access to. Your role is to consolidate lots of information from lots of different sources into a digestible tool that provides impact and proactive recommendations. This requires innovation, critical thinking, creativity, search capacity, regional information sharing, excellent writing skills, and proper time management.

What Comes Next?

In the first two modules, we have discussed two tools to build alignment and strength: defining your *wants* and beginning to build out a professional development plan customized to your analytical and technical skills and talents. Do you feel like you are receiving value? Yes, you are! What are you excited to explore? Finding what drives you? Ironing out your professional development plan? If you are looking for guided support through this process, our team walks you through each of these core competency areas step-by-step so that you have the help you need to achieve your goals!

Success Highlights

Michelle F. joined our **RG** Program and, after working with her coach to align with her true desires, some she never even dreamt of, she gained the freedom to do the fun part of her job, gained financial independence, and built confidence like no one's business! She also took advantage of the technical assistance and was able to transform hours and hours of manual data tabulation for her monthly staff meetings into *one button-click*! She shares, "I set all these goals and smashed them one after the other, including buying a home! I give my agency a better work product because I am happier! The freedom that comes with knowing I have the confidence to get exactly what I want is truly an amazing feeling!" See her story here: https://youtu.be/QgIVLgDP5x0

Inspired Action Exercise

> SUCCESS TIP:
>
> *Build a professional development power plan that catapults your success!*

Now we understand that gaining clarity on what we want in our lives will help us point our compass in the right direction. Next, as analysts, we want to build our analytical capacities. We focus on skill development. We must focus on continuous growth – what vision we have for our futures and what action steps to concentrate on to get there.

The purpose of Module 2 has been to help you create clarity around your current technology and analytical competencies and was designed to help you close the gap between what your analyst strategy is, what your talents are, and what competencies you need to deliver strategic priorities.

We spent time exploring specific skills in each of the types of analysis as well as skills and action steps that all analysts must implement. We run a program that parallels this book, and it offers tools for you related to a variety of evolving skills you require as a great Law Enforcement Analyst. Our program helps you with an assessment of the skill subject area, the details of that skill subject, a column for you to rate your current skill set in each category on a scale of one to ten, one meaning no training or experience in the subject area and ten meaning proficient in the skillset.

You can begin designing your professional development action plan to stay on track when you join our program. Crafting a quality professional development power plan is the first of several proven models of efficiency and success. Establishing an evolving professional development plan is necessary to build confidence, skill set, and marketability. Use the skills detailed in this chapter to start to assess where you are in your growth strategy and gaps that need to be filled. Explore what your mindset is around your own professional development investments and move into a space of continuously learning and growing with intention and direction.

As one of our students, we provide you with a customized plan to achieve accelerated success. Together we review an Analytical Development Planning Matrix. The matrix lets you explore and identify assets and knowledge you may already possess and those you may choose to develop further. Those assets include what is listed above and more!

We go through *all* the skills you need (the above are just examples.) For instance, Intelligence Analysts need to know about specific legal issues relative to data collection and dissemination, specific collection requirements and methodologies, various types of analytics and processes, networking, and other technologies. Analysts must be up-to-date and relevant in the skills and technologies that help them deliver their greatest contributions with confidence and distinction.

We also help you develop a progressive professional development roadmap with timelines plus links to numerous free training resources that align specifically with your growth path—all in one place. Easy peasy. Our programs have tools, assessments, and more to bring the analyst from A to Z in an accelerated process without confusion or overwhelm.

5 Things Analysts Must Do Daily

Excellence in Analytics

My gift to you: Five Things Analysts Must Do Daily

> *What should I be doing as an analyst?*

Your number one goal is *to provide actionable reporting so that your officers, command staff and detectives can succeed.* That means that you are regularly identifying patterns and trends, identifying potential suspect leads, and contributing in an essential way to your agency's operations. Visit your personal mission often! Whether you are new to analysis or a seasoned analyst who needs a boost, these five things are key activities that every analyst needs to do to be the CEO of their analytical role. Check out this free download on <u>5 Things Analysts Must Do</u> (http://bitly.ws/gMwb)

MODULE 3
NURTURE PARTNERSHIPS AND ACHIEVE INFLUENCE

> *"Being a part of the RG programs has improved my confidence in the job I am doing, brought more focus on work/life balance, and has provided amazing tools I can implement to be a better leader and team member. The ability to talk about issues and get ideas on how to be a better leader from other like-minded people in a safe, nonjudgmental environment has been one of the best parts of the program."*
> — PATINA CLEMENTS

Why This Matters

Building relationships is critical in law enforcement analytics, as well as for life beyond law enforcement analysis. Many analysts often find themselves stuck behind their desks with little or no interaction with the patrol and other staff whom they are intending to serve. As a result, analysts are unsure if their products are creating value or being utilized, there is limited buy-in to data-driven strategies, and feedback loops necessary to deliver quality products and services are non-existent. It is imperative that analysts understand that for intelligence to be received fully, the recipient must know, like, and trust the person who produces and delivers the data. In addition, there can be opportunities outside of one's current analytical role that go unrealized because of lack of relationship nurturing. This chapter will walk through key action steps that will build influence, trust, and buy-in between the analyst and the staff served. But first, let's start with a story about building relationships.

I delivered a presentation at a conference a few years ago. During that presentation, an analyst, Kaitlyn, was very engaged, nodding her head, answering, and asking questions. I could tell she enjoyed the materials. After the presentation, she approached me and introduced herself. She noted that she just completed an internship at one of my previous police departments, and she valued that experience. We connected a bit, and then went our separate ways.

After the conference, she reached out via email to follow up. She expressed that she was looking for an entry opportunity in the law enforcement analyst field. I shared a few ideas with her, and she eagerly pursued them. A short time later, I found myself needing someone to do some essential work for my business. I connected with Kaitlyn to see if she'd be interested. She jumped on the opportunity – which was low-paying and not crime analysis-based. She would organize contacts, review webinars for alignment, and perform similar tasks. (She got the goods on the Rising GENIUSS course well before it was published!)

Kaitlyn took these challenges on. She was quick, professional, organized, respectful, kind, and she helped me out quite a bit. At some point, she applied for a job at a local police agency.

Although she had not given me as a reference, the person hiring recognized my name and contacted me, asking about Kaitlyn – her character and work ethic. I gave her a raving review!

Here's a second story that communicates the benefits of building relationships. An undercover narcotics detective was sitting on a vehicle with an unknown male driver in that vehicle. He reached out to me in Crime Analysis and asked what I could tell him about the unknown male. I performed the regular searches of my analytical systems to no avail. Because I continuously nurtured a network of friend analysts, I decided to reach out to them.

Within minutes, an old intern of mine who was now a Gang Intelligence Analyst at the Fusion Center in the bordering state responded with intelligence out of Boston, Massachusetts and shared a responsive contact who could further assist. After reaching out to the Boston Intelligence Unit about said vehicle, they identified the male in the vehicle and noted that he was arrested in a city about 30 miles outside of Boston. Luckily, I had recently attended my monthly regional analyst networking meeting and knew the analyst from that city. Within a few minutes, that analyst was able to share a photo of the arrested individual along with intelligence from her city-based system. It was less than a half hour after the call from my detective that I was able to identify the subject, provide relevant and important intelligence, and create a safer situation for the undercover agent. As you can see, building relationships must be intentional and certainly is fruitful. Now it's time to build your influence and relationships that will support your efforts at your agency and beyond.

Your Best Outcome

Coming up, in Part One of this chapter, we review extensively the five key characteristics of our influence: authenticity, connecting with the core desire of others, personal ownership and accountability, intuition, and finally W. D. Wattles' *Law of the Impression of Increase.* In Part Two of this chapter, we review the Proximity Principle - specifically connecting with people who inspire you to greater achievements, who elevate you. Finally, in Part Three of this chapter, we examine how to build quality relationships.

This module is vital for understanding how to gain industry influence and build a sustainable network of opportunities integral to career and personal growth. It explores who is in our inner circle, who influences us, and who stretches us. Additionally, it highlights the importance of coaches and mentors, masterminding groups, networks, and other platforms that connect you with people who will elevate you. We examine the core characteristics of influence and develop a relationship-building strategy with key partners. After reading this module, you should be able to build more valuable and strategic relationships.

Smart Strategy

Part 1: Characteristics Of Our Influence

What is influence? Influence is the ability to affect a person's behavior in the direction of success. Influence isn't about command or positional power. It's about building effective and quality relationships that expand trust and increase your credibility. Why is this important in law enforcement analysis? Well, creating buy-in with your officers, dispatch, commanders, and even IT staff involves developing trust. How do you do that? Working through these specific characteristics will start you on that journey.

Influence in your department is just as significant as influence outside of your department. Being influential among your peers, social groups, and industry could lead you to the biggest opportunity of your life. Let's begin.

Characteristic #1: Authenticity

Being authentic starts with being genuine, trustworthy, confident, and honest. An authentic person is thoughtful, expresses emotions clearly, and learns from mistakes. Importantly, authenticity consists of being self-aware and honestly expressing your vulnerabilities with the right audience. To be credible and authentic in building relationships, you must take a genuine interest in others.

How do you become genuinely interested in other people? Have you ever noticed the answer to the question, "How are you?" is a generic, "Great"? Do you ever feel that people don't care what your response is? Nobody is waiting for you to say, "Well, actually, I'm having a tough day. I'm fighting with my husband, I feel bloated, and my work is stressing me out!" Do *you* ask the question, "How are you?" and not listen to the response? One of the facets of being authentic is that you take the time and energy to listen actively. Become more intentional in this area. Try asking a question referencing something specific. Say, "Hey Jane. I know you were having a rough time last week on the report. Did you end up working through those

Excel charts?" Or, "Hey Mike, I saw on your Facebook post that you decided to run a marathon. Congrats! Are you following a specific training plan?" These are examples of connecting authentically, provided you are genuinely interested in their responses. Being truly authentic is a characteristic that will bring you closer to developing quality relationships and gaining influence.

Characteristic #2: Connecting With The Core Desire Of Others

To influence others to act, we must first connect with a core desire within them. Let me share a story with you from Dale Carnegie's book, *How to Influence People in the Digital Age.* One day, the famous philosopher Ralph Waldo Emerson and his son tried to get a calf into the barn because they wanted to have lunch. They pushed and pulled and yelled. Yet the calf would not return to the barn. Ralph and his son were frustrated.

A humble housemaid without brilliant books or academic credentials thought she might be able to resolve the problem. She knew that the calf's core desire was food and that tapping into that core desire would influence the calf's response. The housemaid offered the calf her finger, which reminded the calf that some warm milk was nearby. The calf quickly entered the barn. This story shows that influence requires more intuition than intellect. It requires us to know what people truly want and desire. If we look at challenges from another person's perspective, we begin to see solutions from a different lens, leading to achieving buy-in and influence.

Characteristic #3: Personal Ownership and Accountability

Taking ownership means being accountable for something entirely yours. Everything that happens in that situation is your responsibility. As the CEO of Crime Analysis (Yes! You are the CEO of your analytical role!) who demonstrates ownership, you have an emotional investment in your work, team, success, and failures. Ownership is recognized when you go above and beyond what you are strictly accountable for, regardless of being recognized or compensated for that intention. You don't give excuses or point the finger – instead, you overcome obstacles and get things done. This sense of reliability and accountability creates influence.

Characteristic #4: Intuition

Rely on your inner voice, your gut instinct, to help make decisions with clarity and awareness. You can understand a situation immediately without the need for conscious reasoning. Some studies show that the intuitive part of our brain knows the correct answer long before the analytical part of our brain. This dichotomy can be a challenge, especially for analysts, as we are trained to analyze, over-analyze, and then analyze some more! Yet we have all heard the phrase, 'analysis paralysis.' Over-analysis appears as indecisiveness and lack of confidence in the analyst's product and self. Using your intuition effectively can create trust from within as well as from those around you. There are many ways to improve our intuition that can augment our brains in analytical decision-making and essentially lead to deeper connections and quality relationships, thus more influence. Here are just a few ways to work on our intuition: ask questions and listen for the answer, envision a conversation with a wise mentor, quiet your mind for three minutes several times a day.

You are the expert. You are the analyst. You are the CEO of analysis. You can create excellence. When you believe this, others will also accept it. And then comes influence.

Characteristic #5: The Law of the Impression of Increase

The *Law of the Impression of Increase* is a key to your success and is based on the concepts of prosperity, abundance, and increase. In *How to Get What You Want*, Wallace D. Wattles states, "Every word and act will convey the idea of advancement and increase to others, and they will be drawn to you. Always remember that what all people are seeking for is to increase." By making a habit of creating more for others (more value, more quality, just 'more,') our lives will be happier and more productive, and we gain influence. It's important to remember that creating "more" for others is done without expecting something in return.

Here are some ideas on how to create an impression of increase with everyone we meet. These are simple but go a long, long way.

- Start looking for what other people do well. Bring it to their attention. Let them know that you notice.
- Smile at everyone.
- Give sincere compliments and praise.
- Congratulate your officers on their successes.
- Help others succeed.
- Give your commanders an idea that inspires them.

- Give gifts physically, verbally, and emotionally.
- Offer opportunities for advancement and development.
- Highlight others' successes at meetings or in front of others.
- Give another person something of greater value than what they paid for it.

Authenticity, connecting with the core desire of others, personal ownership and accountability, using our intuition, and leaving others with the impression of an increase are just a few of the core factors of influence. Creating influence starts from creating quality within yourself. And once you tune into that, others will be drawn to you and your influence.

Part 2: The Proximity Principle - Connect With People Who Elevate You

Here we examine who is in our inner circle, who influences us, and who stretches us to grow. We look at coaches and mentors, mastermind groups, and other platforms that connect us with people who understand us, who relate to our aspirations, who are like-minded around values and goals.

Far too often, we keep toxic people and environments in our lives for one reason or another. It's imperative that we create boundaries and intentionally cut out those who are not serving us in a healthy way.

Who are the leaders in your life who elevate you? Who are the people who lift you to a higher level? Every time you leave them, you feel energized, motivated, and inspired, like hearing a motivational speaker and feeling ready to conquer anything. (Maybe you feel this at our weekly 'boost' sessions?

Tribe of Excellence-
https://www.facebook.com/groups/171925267401670)

These can be 'rocket boosters' you know personally or someone distant from you whom you admire. These people are our primary support system, and they nurture our future successes. They are brilliant in areas where we are still growing. They inspire us, stretch us, and call us to our greatness. These people and groups pour light into us, amplify us, and bring us to greater prosperity. We must intentionally bring ourselves into proximity with the people who encourage us to step outside our comfort zone. We gain belief in ourselves and our abilities when we align ourselves with top achievers, rocket boosters, leaders, and catalysts of positive change. These can be coaches, mentors, mastermind groups, co-workers, family, friends, or volunteers.

Proximity to the right people and places positions us where we *need* to be and propels us to where we *want* to be. Don't over-complicate the journey. Quiet the fear and doubt. Meet great people who will lead you to other great people and opportunities. Position yourself so opportunities can find you. Leaders are constantly scanning – books, podcasts, YouTube speeches – and asking, "*Whom do I need to be around, and where do I need to be to grow?*" Do the same.

We have discussed two tools so far to build partnerships and influence: characteristics of influencers and the proximity principle – aligning yourself with people and environments that cause you to grow. Do you feel like you are receiving value? What are you excited to explore? Diving into the core characteristics of influence? Connecting with those who elevate you? We will continue to walk through each of these pillars step-by-step so that you have the support you need to achieve your goals!

Part 3: Build Quality Relationships

The last part of Module 3 is building quality relationships. Things are going to happen because of the relationships we build. It may be right away, or it may be years down the road. The idea is to continuously build quality relationships as they lead to other quality relationships and opportunities and even a higher quality life!

Say no to "networking" and yes to connections. Have you ever been to a networking event where you felt like you met 100 people but never actually "connected" with anyone? Maybe you attended a conference or convention and felt lost in the sea of people. Well, I permit you to *never* attend a networking event again! That's right. Never again! Instead, seek out events and opportunities that will give you space to build relationships. At these events, set a connection goal to connect with three new people. I don't mean pass out your card or stalk someone. I mean, really, truly connect.

Relationship-Building Strategy

Here are some ideas for relationship-building that will lead to genuine connections:

1. Ask to grab a coffee together after a meeting.
2. Visit each other's police agencies.
3. Help on a project.
4. Get out of your office and go to all roll call sessions.
5. Go to a community event.

6. Co-create a presentation for your local networking group or an IACA conference.
7. Volunteer at a personal event.
8. Send a snail mail card to a friend.
9. Go on a ride-along with a patrol officer.
10. Reach out personally when you see something happening on social media (versus just "liking" or commenting.)

Again, things are going to happen because of the relationships we build. It may not be right away but the relationships we build, and *how* we build them, provide quality connections and future opportunities.

Recap

You now have three concepts - influence, connection, and relationships - that will bring you closer to being an excellent analyst and *leader of self.* You discovered five key characteristics of influence, including authenticity, connecting with the core desire of others, personal ownership, and accountability, using your intuition, and leaving others with the impression of increase. Also, you learned about connecting with 'rocket boosters' – aligning with those people and environments that elevate you. Finally, you learned some techniques to build quality relationships, just like Kaitlyn did with me.

I know that this may feel exciting and a little overwhelming at the same time. No worries – the program we offer, which parallels the modules in this book, seamlessly takes you through, step-by-step, these success habits and more to genuinely shift your results in a positive direction. Right now, take time each day this week to explore and touch upon what you've learned from reading. You don't have to do them all at once. Each time you dive in, you dive deeper into your personal growth!

Success Highlights

Put your hands together for RG member Jenn Z. who recently saw an enormous triumph! She is a newer analyst to her agency (under two years at the time of this story), trying to gain buy-in from her peers and the staff she serves. We all know this can be a big challenge! She was trying to figure out a way to use the intelligence information from area agencies and essential to her detectives. With the help of her coach, she developed an Access database to store this info and deliver automated actionable reports and investigative leads. She didn't stop there! Knowing how vital buy-in is, she developed a feedback loop with detectives to help determine what works best in terms of analysis and reporting, and they met to discuss progress. They brainstormed ways to make it better and support detectives and officers. AND... she recruited two detectives to be her guinea pigs and to start building stories! As a result, the team invited her to their lineups and presented her intelligence insight weekly. Jenn recommends getting to know your officers and detectives personally - like working out together - and discussing non-work activities. She says that getting to know them better personally (and they, her) makes their work conversations and growth so much easier. Congrats, Jenn, for this and all your successes as a repeat RG member!

Inspired Action Exercise

Rocket Boosters

Who are the leaders in your life who encourage you? Who are the people that lift you to a higher level? Every time you leave them, you feel energized, motivated, and inspired. These can be 'rocket boosters' you know personally or someone you admire from a distance. And since this is a book about career *and* personal joy, consider rocket boosters in your professional network as well as those in your personal world.

As an exercise, first write the names of three influencers/rocket boosters whom you admire. Reflect on what you like about them... what qualities they have that you admire. Note the life area that they best support. For example, I chose three people:

Rocket Booster: Dave Ramsey, a public figure

What I admire about him: He has a deep passion for helping others to become debt-free. He has an excellent financial sense, is to the point, and sticks to what is right even if others don't agree.

Life Area: Financial success and legacy

Rocket Booster: Holly, a friend

What I admire about her:

Holly is such a savvy businesswoman who seems to connect authentically with so many people. She went to Africa, led a biking team across the country, and thinks so out of the box! I admire her incredible sense of intuition, the fact that she doesn't care what others think, and she always takes a bit out of life.

Life Area: Business and Friendship

Rocket Booster: Personal Coach, a professional influence

What I admire about her: I admire that my coach seems to always draw out the best in me. I always feel excited after talking with her. She knows the field so well and offers me tremendous insight.

Life Area: Business

Now it's your turn - think of people who encourage you and run through the exercise!

My Rocket Booster is -

Why I Admire Them is -

The Life Area They Impact is -

1.

2.

3.

Build Relationships

Next, establish a relationship-building technique specific to the individuals you chose. Refer to the list earlier in the chapter for ideas to nurture these relationships.

Example: You have identified Carol as a key field leader from a local police agency. You call Carol to let her know you enjoyed her presentation on the gang investigation. You advise her you are working on a similar issue in your department and that seeing her process in person could help you. You ask to visit her for one hour and experience what she does to support her command staff. You bring her tea to thank her for her time (because you found out she doesn't like coffee.)

Building

Relationships

Analyst tool for building quality
relationships & buy-in

My gift to you: Building Relationships

Law enforcement analysts and supervisors can use this tool to build high-quality relationships in your career and in your personal life. Note that relationship-building should be intertwined into the daily schedule of an analyst both with personal and with professional connections. Here are some free tools to get you started!

Building Relationships Free Download (https://bit.ly/2YapgvE)

MODULE 4
INSTALL SYNERGY AND PRODUCTIVITY HABITS

> *"The resources EIA provided not only helped me to feel confident in the technical skills needed to create actionable products, but also encouraged me to clarify the purpose behind these products so that my time was used with more intention and resulted in greater impact."*
> — ELIZABETH ANDERSON

Why This Matters

Welcome to Module 4 - so proud of you! We have done much work so far! Let's just take a moment and reflect. We have aligned with our purpose, skills, talents, and passions. We have defined the fundamental technology and analytical skills we want to develop further. We have discovered five principal characteristics of influence, including authenticity, connecting with the core desire of others, personal ownership, accountability using your intuition, and leaving others with the impression of increase (Wallace D. Wattles). We learned about connecting with 'rocket boosters' - aligning with those people and environments that lift us to new heights. And finally, we learned some techniques to build quality relationships. I trust that you are starting to see the bigger picture and working to apply these pivotal skills to help you find your genius as a law enforcement analyst while you equally value work-life harmony.

In this module we will debunk three high performance myths, we will cover three steps involved in a Productivity Audit, and we will wrap up with an unveiling of four productivity hacks that will save you time, energy, and your sanity. Are you ready? Let's start with the myths!

Peak Performance Myths

As professionals, it is crystal clear to us that data can help drive decisions. We see, for instance, if we examine the last three to five years of trend data, we can develop strategies and deploy resources much more precisely and efficiently. We understand and value the importance of data-driven strategies.... But are we hypocrites?

Let me share a true story with you by Price Pritchett from his book "You Squared. Create Your Quantum Leap Strategy" *(Pritchett & Associates Rep Edition. February 1, 2012)*

Price was sitting in a private room, a peaceful place hidden back among the pine trees about an hour from Toronto. It was just past noon, late July, and he was listening to the desperate sounds of a life-or-death struggle going on a few feet away.

> "There's a small fly burning out the last of its short life's energies in a futile attempt to fly through the glass of the windowpane. The whining wings tell the poignant story of the fly's strategy—*try harder*. But it's not working. The

frenzied effort offers no hope for survival. Ironically, the *struggle is part of the trap*. It is impossible for the fly to try hard enough to succeed at breaking through the glass. Nevertheless, this little insect has staked its life on reaching its goal through *raw effort and determination*. This fly is doomed. It will die there on the windowsill. Across the room, ten steps away, the door is open. Ten seconds of flying time, and this small creature could reach the outside world it seeks. With only a fraction of the effort now being wasted, it could be free of this self-imposed trap. The breakthrough possibility is there. It would be *so easy*. Why doesn't the fly try another approach, something dramatically different? How did it get so locked in on the idea that this particular route, and determined effort, offer the most promise for success? What logic is there in continuing, until death, to seek a breakthrough with "more of the same"? No doubt this approach makes sense to the fly. Regrettably, it's an idea that will kill. *"Trying harder" isn't necessarily the solution to achieving more.* It may not offer any real promise for getting what you want out of life. Sometimes, in fact, it's a *big part of the problem*. If you stake your hopes for a breakthrough on trying harder than ever, you may kill your chances for success."

Are you like the fly, constantly pushing harder and harder instead of smarter? Are you reactive to the way we describe our officers? Reactive to phone calls, data requests, negative habits, and attitudes that force us to continue our struggles with no promise of success?

Let's find out. Let's play a fun little game. You decide if you are the fly that is repeatedly slamming against the window or if you are the fly who sees the door wide open. Put a checkmark next to the following statements that apply to you or your team:

- Do you find that you are constantly stressed about how and when to spend your time?
- Are you overwhelmed?
- Are you such a perfectionist that you get stuck on tasks for days?
- Do you find yourself sitting at your desk for hours working on what feels like never-ending assignments?
- Do you constantly feel as if your laundry list of to-dos is long and unattainable?
- Do you regularly take work home or opt to work on a vacation day so that you have quiet to get work done?
- Are you stuck choosing which priority should be done first? Do you feel disorganized and unproductive?
- Do you feel as if you are constantly working on inconsequential requests rather than performing the quality analytics you desire?
- Do you spend your time on projects that feel irrelevant to you?
- Do you wish you had tools in place to automate repetitive work?
- Do you regularly participate in meaningless meetings, discussions, phone calls, or even web surfing?
- Do you spend time responding to unimportant emails?
- Do you wake up and check email or Facebook first thing in the morning?

- Are you reactive? Are you productive or just busy? Does high-level work take a back seat because you respond to emails, return phone calls, or run reports?

The goal here is to help you discover ways to decrease the unnecessary work you perform while increasing productivity. Our coaching programs *dig deep* into multiple efficiency habits such as the Pomodoro ® Technique, time chunking, setting priorities, automation techniques, compounding habits, performing efficiency audits, and more. Highly effective and successful people create goals and get focused. Let's take a look at how they do that.

There are three fundamental *myths* we must understand:

1. To-Do Lists are a MYTH!

Far too often, we generate generic lists of what we need to do, primarily based on reactive requests and our desire to check things off, and the lists can feel never-ending. Often, we spend time on the items easiest to achieve and delay focusing on our priorities that will deliver greater impact. Instead, create "Success Lists," or lists that start with a goal and are engineered to include only those action steps that reach results. Success lists provide a more strategic means to structure and focus analytic efforts on actionable outcomes.

2. Multi-tasking is a MYTH!

Neuroscience research has shown that the brain does not perform two tasks simultaneously but instead starts and stops at each task. Professionals who multi-task are spreading themselves too thin and not deeply engaging in analytics that could produce exceptional results.

3. Work and work and work some more is a MYTH!

Working harder does not produce long-term results. It causes unnecessary stress on the body and mind and leads to burnout, fatigue, and frustration. Consider an athlete in training. He trains consistently and persistently yet knows recovery is a central component to his time spent training. Professionals must consider the same and incorporate recovery as a primary component in peak performance.

Productivity Audit Step 1: Take Inventory

Now that we understand the baseline concepts, we can begin our steps to our Productivity Audit. The first step is identifying and understanding the responsibilities we currently have. Begin by taking inventory of what your day/week/month looks like. Get out a piece of paper and jot down a dump of everything you are responsible for doing. Include the specifics of all tasks now and in the future. As you work through this section, be as specific as possible regarding the audience, the type of report, type of training, etc. Below are some examples to help you begin to think about your responsibilities and priorities.

- Weekly reports
- Meeting with team
- Respond to complex and straightforward data requests
- Personal growth and training

Many professionals who have gone through this process before discovered that they are doing a great deal of work, yet much of it is unnecessary with little future focus. They feel overwhelmed, undervalued, and often burned out. They also discover that much of their energy is fractured, geared towards putting out fires and responding to requests. This reactive mode is true for supervisors, individuals, and teams alike.

Do you identify as someone who is stuck in reactive mode? Or are you taking a proactive approach to your role, fulfilling your goal to provide actionable opportunities for your agency to succeed? Wherever you are today is exactly where you need to be. Our goal through these modules and accompanying course is to move you and your teams to peak performance, proactive time and priority management, and effective and valued contributions to your industry. You are just beginning to change and improve!

Your Best Outcome

We are here to permanently free you from reactivity!

Installing synergy and productivity habits is critical for creating simple practices and efficiencies to bring you to the highest level of productivity and *wellness* in your career! You are about to discover methods for getting more quality work done in less time, expediting the achievement of your goals, building cohesive teams, and creating the work-life harmony you seek and deserve.

Smart Strategy

Productivity Audit Step 2: Prioritize Your Success List

The next step to multiply your effectiveness is to prioritize your success list. We shift from "to-do lists" to a much more strategic approach that considers results over tactics. There are two key concepts to keep in mind as you prioritize your success list and your team's efforts.

Productivity Audit Step 2, Key Concept 1: Setting Goals and Maintaining Focus

Two fundamentals of becoming more productive are *setting goals* and *maintaining focus.* People and groups with clear goals outperform groups without explicit goals. A big mistake professionals make is creating reactive to-do lists - they have a *quantity* expectation versus a *quality* expectation. To become more effective, we must limit our distractions while increasing the outputs that matter. Establishing priorities that support a vision of the utility of yourself and your team is essential.

'Success Lists' mandate that you must know where you are going first. You then create action steps to help you reach those goals. If you discover your to-do list items are not linked to a bigger goal, then adjust now. Think about the bigger picture goal and determine which activities align with that goal. For instance, if your goal is to achieve a certification, what specific action step must you reverse engineer to accomplish that goal? You would not take every free, random training that came your way. Instead, you would identify the needed criteria for said certification and then reserve two hours per week to complete the requirements for certification.

Similarly, suppose your goal is to provide actionable reporting weekly relative to emerging patterns and trends to influence strategies. Now your priority shifts from responding to community data requests and attending peripheral meetings. Your priorities shift to reading reports, studying data for emerging patterns, creating threshold automation, attending briefings regularly to report on such patterns, assisting in strategy development, and other activities necessary for the outcome you chose. Point your compass accurately to follow action steps that move you towards the identified goal.

Productivity Audit Step 2, Key Concept 2: Take breaks!

We talked about this in our productivity myths conversation above; active recovery should be, but is rarely, incorporated into a strategic efficiency design. Many professionals feel the need to 'power through' instead of considering self-care as essential to their success. Lacking *leadership of self* - putting in longer hours, skipping breaks, eating lunch in front of the computer, picking up the phone at all hours of the day and night - is rarely the correct response.

If you want to feel more energized, creative, and effective at work - and end your day with enough oomph for your 'life' outside of work - you must prioritize *leadership of self* first. This means that you schedule breaks, vacations, lunches, physical activity, meditation, and other types of *leadership of self* activities throughout your day. Ideally, stop your work and give your mind and body a break every forty-five to sixty minutes. *(High Performance Habits by* Brendon Burchard*).* Breaks do *not* mean checking email, texts, or social media. Instead, we need to 'check out' so we can recharge! If you are a supervisor, please consider setting the pace and culture for your team. I encourage you to build *leadership of self* as your *first* priority!

Productivity Audit Step 3: "Time Chunking"

This step optimizes results with the concepts of habits, assessment, and time organization. Much research indicates that small habits implemented consistently yield the most significant changes. Getting one percent better each day has a compound effect over time. In addition, if you do not always measure the major areas and goals of your life, you will not be able to see progress or adjust to create efficiencies and balance. The next time you want to make a change, decide to make a small change for a week and assess your progress. Then compound, or add, a small change on top of that for another week. Then evaluate and adjust again. Continue this process for sixty-six days, and voilà! A positive habit is formed! You now set priorities and proactively 'chunk time.' The more we iterate, the better we get. To get started, do the following:

- Get out a physical or digital calendar and block off your time in one-hour chunks.
- Be sure to include ten minutes between projects to rest and regroup.
- Insert the *priorities* listed from previous steps, including time to automate a task, train someone else on tasks you are releasing, etc.
- Add white space, personal care, breaks, time for unplanned events (building relationships, self-care.)
- Add a time block on Fridays after lunch called "Productivity Review" (or for supervisors - "Strategic

Thinking.") Assess what did and didn't work. Plan, and adjust the following week accordingly. Where did you go over your time? What tasks could you have eliminated? What self-care did you implement? Did you focus on the priorities you decided in advance were important? Were you able to adjust if a new important request/task came in unexpectedly? What did you let go of? How do you feel? Next, set up your 'time chunk' schedule for the following week.

Notably, the field of law enforcement analytics often has varying schedules, emergency activities (such as a new homicide case,) and other critical demands that must allow for flexibility in scheduling. However, don't use this as an excuse to jump from project to project or blur your boundaries. There are two pieces of advice I have for you to keep you on track when these events occur. (1) Be flexible for emergencies or assignments outside of your planning but recognize what is a true emergency versus someone else's circus. (2) Focus on achieving impact. That impact may not always fit into a specific time slot but starting your day with the intention of completing a project that brings impact will help you align with the activities that support that specific desired impact. That means stop getting the little things done first because they are easier to check off. Instead, decide on the one thing that you can do to move the needle on an impact-producing activity. Then do it!

Productivity Hacks

Now it is time to discover how to maximize your time during the assigned time blocks or purpose-driven days. Here are four hacks to get you started.

Productivity Hack #1: Pomodoro Technique

We will start with the Pomodoro Technique. The Pomodoro Technique is a time management system that encourages people to work with the time they have—rather than against it. At the beginning of the day, choose three main achievements ("Success List") to accomplish. It is vital to invest time choosing three things to do daily to move you closer to your goals. Write them down. For instance, let's say your priority is completing an analysis/report that will drive your agency decisions. Decide three things today that you must do to get you closer to the goal: (1) gather the needed information and create storylines, (2) identify and analyze data, and (3) create an actionable report that you will use to drive strategy.

The next step is to get all your supplies ready (stickies, laptops, access to the database, etc.). Shut off email and social media. Turn off the internet. Shut the door or throw on some headphones. Silence your phone - *and* flip it over!

Now you are ready. Set your intention before every single task. For instance, set the intention that you are going to read the 50 new reports from Friday and create storylines in your database for each within the next 45 minutes. This will get you closer to your goal of identifying any emerging patterns. Work on the first topic with intention and focus for the next 45 minutes. Decide that within these 45 minutes, you will achieve this goal! If you feel yourself getting off track, remind yourself that this is the *one thing* you must accomplish during this time segment to be satisfied with your accomplishment. Speed read your reports, make notes of things to research during your next Pomodoro cycle, identify possible related reports, and stay on task.

When the 45-minute buzzer goes off, you *must stop.* Do not finish. Do not extend the time. *Stop* and take a five to ten-minute break. Get up. Stretch. Move your body. Science supports that your body and mind work best when incorporating recovery into your performance strategy.

Repeat the cycle two times with specific tasks in mind. For your last 45 minutes, grab a template and incorporate your findings. Make it a short, sweet, actionable, and 'red-light-ready' report. Remember, it is not about perfection. It is about providing accurate and timely analytics that help your agency find opportunities for success.

The stages of planning, tracking, recording, processing, and visualizing are fundamental to the Pomodoro Technique. In the planning phase, you record a "Success List," noting the top activities that *must be completed* (or at least begun) that day. The technique's premise is that the timer instills a sense of urgency. Rather than squandering work hours on distractions, you recognize you are constrained to 45 minutes to make as much progress on a task as possible. The timer also reminds you to get up and take a breather. The process is designed for you to get focused. Get intentional. And take breaks.

Additionally, the forced breaks help cure that frazzled, burnt-out feeling most of us experience toward the end of the day. This cycle has been proven in hundreds of research articles and certainly in my own life. I encourage you to schedule your intention and your breaks as mandatory parts of your day.

Productivity Hack #2: Walk Away from Your Computer

So many professionals are chained to their desks, working incredibly hard, often resulting in burnout! *Leadership of self* is essential; it must be a priority! This is where work-life integration is created. Trust me... the work will always be there. Your health, your family, your sanity will not!

Productivity Hack #3: Limit Email, Phone, And Social Media Consumption

Now that you are the CEO of your career and your life, it is up to you to define and implement effective efficiency habits, including limiting your distractions. Tim Ferris's book, *The Four-Hour Workweek,* digs into this in detail. He emphasizes creating healthy boundaries that empower others, free up your own time, and create a culture of ownership. For optimized performance, check your email, phone messages, and social media two to three times per day, at noon and four pm or at 10 am, 1 pm and 4 pm. This creates tons of gray space for high-priority tasks without interruption. First create an email response. If you are freaking out right now, propose a three-to-five-day trial to see how this can work with and for your managers. I promise you, many reluctant professionals and supervisors who gave this a try experienced improved workflow and focus immediately.

Here is a simple email template from Ferris' book, altered to fit law enforcement analytics:

Greetings,

Our priority is to provide actionable insight for the strategic growth of XXX agency. I check and respond to emails three times a day at 10 am, 1 pm, and 4 pm Eastern to serve you best. If you require urgent assistance (please ensure that it is urgent) that cannot wait until 10 am, 1 pm, or 4 pm, please contact me via phone at 555-555-5555. Thank you for understanding this move to more efficiency and effectiveness. It helps me accomplish more and serve you better.

Sincerely,
Your Name

You may set up a similar voice mail, place a "Do Not Disturb" sign at your door or cubicle, or have headphones on (even if you are not playing anything) during chunks of time when you desire absolute silence to concentrate. During such focus periods, batch your activities. For instance, if you know that you receive requests all week long, plan to push out all non-urgent requests for two hours each Thursday. Imagine how it will feel to be free from meaningless and frustrating interruptions!

Productivity Hack #4: Design Automation Processes

Every professional must streamline repetitive processes and automate activities. There are a variety of automation strategies available for free in a basic Microsoft license. Macros in Microsoft Access and Excel allow you to automate specific tasks by programming a set of one or more actions that produce a particular result. For instance, you can set up macros to run all append queries to add new data to your master databases each day or automate the ten queries that create your monthly summary reports. You get the idea! Your life is about to get simpler!

Michelle from Tyler, Texas, is a professional who implemented an automation strategy successfully. Michelle consumed several hours every two weeks producing a report. It was manually intensive and, quite honestly, made her feel like pulling her hair out! We sat together and implemented a couple of automation techniques. Now that report takes her 120 seconds to complete! She recovered six hours she can apply to making other valuable contributions to the agency!

Your Action Steps

1. Write a list of anything that you do on a repetitive basis. Identify ways to automate them. Plug *automation* time into your time-chunking schedule now!
2. Identify a plan to learn automation strategies. Here are some other links and tools that you can use to begin to think about how to automate your processes:

- Free resources in our tribe of excellence Facebook community: https://bit.ly/2WptDCf
- Automation tools in our RG program: https://bit.ly/39OrJhv
- Free automation series (IADLEST): https://bit.ly/3kOt4v4

I trust that you are well on your way to implementing systems that will help you become *more productive* and *less busy...and less stressed!* You now recognize the various performance myths and are equipped with the tools you need to identify priorities, claim your time, and implement performance strategies that produce high-quality results. Multiplying your productivity takes intention, planning, evaluation, persistence, and commitment to self-leadership. It requires you to visit, revisit, implement, shift, grow, and iterate again! We invite you to participate in a live Peak Productivity Masterclass privately or with others who will ignite and elevate you. Please visit our Tribe of Excellence Facebook community for the next free, live session or reach out to schedule a private session for you and your team.

- Tribe of Excellence FB community for next live session: https://bit.ly/2WptDCf

Success Highlights

Dianna F. participated in our RG program and then graduated into our RG Leaders Program. After just a few short months, Dianna saw tremendous progress as she established her open database connection to her RMS/CAD, developed a master crime analysis database, linked all her tables, and set up many queries and reports! This effort took months of determination and conversations to get the connection and sweat and tears building the back end! As a result, Diana now has easy and accurate access to her data and *trusts* her system! No more pulling data from a dumpy RMS export. No more manually typing data into Excel. No more not being able to answer in-depth questions about cases or people or patterns. Diana now can automate reports, dig into her data with ease, and identify patterns and trends. Diana put her CEO hat on and is delivering what her agency needs in this capacity and leading her unit in other infrastructure growth areas. They are so lucky to have her! Congrats Diana!

Inspired Action Exercise

- Go through the productivity audit and activities presented in this chapter.
- Shift your mindset on productivity and high-performance habits.
- Take inventory and prioritize your "Success List".
- Time chunk and be flexible.
- Implement the four Productivity Hacks.
- Attend the next free, live Peak Productivity Masterclass.
- If you are a supervisor, request the Supervisor's Toolkit (Behind the Scenes) to use during our next live Peak Productivity Masterclass. This is a tool for supervisors to utilize with their teams in unison with the live Peak Productivity Masterclasses. Registration required.
- Listen to the full Productivity Masterclass Recording on YouTube: https://bit.ly/2XWGCvu
- Choose one or two productivity habits from above to implement today and commit for 66 days to ensure the productivity habit will stick! Describe what this will look like. What steps will you take to make this happen consistently? What will success look like for you?
- Join our Facebook page (Tribe of Excellence, https://bit.ly/3upcODT) for inspiration and community.
- Grab your free Goal Crafting recording and worksheet: https://bit.ly/3m8QzhJBonus Tip: Friday Planning Sessions

Decide the Friday before your week what you want to achieve and plug the activities into your schedule. Start with writing a list of all the activities you must complete – those urgent ones and the bigger-picture work (personal development, efforts on a long-term project, connecting, etc.) Next, eliminate those activities that no longer serve you. Then, you can chunk similar activities together. For instance, if you have several colleges requesting you to produce yearly statistics, you can consolidate all their requests into a block. When you set time parameters, your energy is more focused, and you are much more productive. Be sure to add time for lunch *away* from your desk, connecting with others, or chipping away at learning a new skill. Finally, insert some time for creating an automation!

Product Assessment Template

Analyst tool for measuring productivity

My gift to you: Product Assessment Template

> *How do I balance multiple and competing priorities?*

First, get a handle on all the products you produce and the activities you do. Use this Product Assessment Template (https://bit.ly/3idOakT)

to help. This tool helps analysts and supervisors measure the productivity of activities and products, identifies gaps in impact, and provides ideas for filling those gaps.

Second, check yourself! Are you wasting time? Are you performing repetitive tasks and not saving enough time for actual analytics? Installing productivity habits is critical in creating simple habits and efficiencies that will bring you to the highest level of productivity. Analysts must focus on getting more quality work done in less time, accelerating you closer to your goals, and creating that work-life harmony you seek. Attend a free Peak Productivity Masterclass in our Tribe of Excellence (https://bit.ly/3unAad6)

Facebook community to determine if you are focusing on the wrong things. Or reach out to request a private session for you and your team.

Third, review your job description in detail. Consider updating according to current priorities relative to the *impact* that you and your agency desire. Our RG Program (https://bit.ly/3ikopiJ) provides templates for new job descriptions that are actionable, purpose-focused, and will attract the correct type of analyst.

MODULE 5

UNCOVER CONFIDENCE AND SELF-CARE

> *"Dawn taught me not only how to do the job itself, but how to be CONFIDENT and PROUD of the work I put forward."*
> — KERI LEBEAU

Why This Matters

Wow! Can you believe all that you have devoured over the past four chapters! You have learned how to align with your purpose, skills, and passion. You have identified key technology and analytical skills to build upon to grow your skillset, influence, and confidence. You've learned fun ways to save time and create efficiencies. Are you taking action? If not, what's stopping you?

For many people, it's a lack of confidence. Sometimes you have the tools and systems right in front of you, but you can't build up the nerve to *do* something with them. I remember a time when this happened to me; my confidence drained to an all-time low from a bad relationship. Until then, I had been known as the strong, confident young woman - taking risks, excelling in school and sports, purchasing houses, and raising a child as a single mom. I always had a smile on my face. I saw the good or the silver lining in everything and whatever I didn't know, I learned. I even sold my townhouse with nothing but a newspaper advertisement, warm chocolate chip cookies, and an attorney! I felt I could achieve anything if I worked hard and smart. That is until my confidence took a dive.

Here's my story

I was a professional woman civilian in policing, paid higher than any other in my position. For that I was thankful, but careful. From the front lines, I was asked which brass I had lain with as surely a woman civilian could not have climbed that far up without dipping. From the brass, I was given the weekly task of proving (in writing!) my value, sometimes sitting at the oval table, and sometimes tucked in the corner, depending on the chief and number of brass suits in the room. Regardless, I was always the only woman there, minus the secretary taking notes. I sometimes asked myself if I was good enough to be there but hid that fear behind my own suit, busyness, and permanent smile. I stood on my platform of honor and integrity and perfection – hiding any weakness that would make them (or me) sense the insecurity. My mask was practiced often and soon, semi-permanent.

This constant coverup was loud in my personal life, too. I was always the strong one, the one family and friends went to for an ear or solutions. Hardly reciprocated as somehow that would reveal the imposter I truly was. I had achieved so much in just 30-ish years of life – an accelerated bachelor's/master's degree paid in full and Dean's listed, the purchase and sale of multiple homes, a great career, and all while climbing up from being a single, teen mom at 18 years of age with my first child. I knew I should be proud, and was to some extent, but always found myself needing more proof of my value and less pointers to any weakness hidden behind my mask.

I was reluctant to date as somehow it would slow my progress to be an incredible mom and career woman. But soon I found myself head-over-heels in love with a man who made my heart flutter... and my eyes tear often. After the birth of my second daughter, I proclaimed the fluttering heart but hid the daily tears behind my perfection mask as the dichotomy confused and angered me and created this impossible internal struggle. I found myself battling in a difficult relationship, one that I was embarrassed that I had allowed myself to be involved with in the first place.

You see, I read reports regularly about domestic violence and, in a sense, had been desensitized to my own chaos as those reports were "worse" than mine. I deployed officers to these domestic situations yet at home, I endured bed sheets ripped off me in the middle of the night, an elbow to the back because that didn't leave any marks, and the deep, sorrowful guilt of being a bad mother for staying. I only wished he would have left a black and blue bruise, evidence that the turmoil was not all in my head. But he never did. So, I remained silent, unable to reveal my "weakness" to family, friends, or the suits. I felt so weak and alone.

One desperate night at 10 P.M., I lowered my mask and frantically called my dear friends who had a packing crew ready in what felt like an hour. Soon after he declared his determination to make my life hell and did so using his endless supply of money, a high-paid lawyer, and the emotional hooks he still had in my weakened heart. My two girls and I slowly started our new lives in a new state, a restraining order signed – still afraid of him, of being found out, of being flawed.

After years of building and recovering, keeping somewhat silent in my personal struggles, I began to feel like I had turned a corner. I felt strong - my "weakness" accepted by those I loved and undiscovered by the rest. I did not realize it then but upon reflection and experience now see that much of my fear was simply in my head. My friends and family and likely my professional family would have accepted me and perhaps supported me should I have given them the chance earlier.

We were in and out of court, draining my bank account and ego while his remained supple. I felt depleted, but hopeful that the female judge would see my strength and resilience, would award proper child support and visitation schedules, and would put this dishonorable man in his place. But she did not. She awarded him limited child support, as I was the breadwinner on paper, and granted him three weekend visits per month. Since my parenting time was during the week and, according to the court I chose to work during that parenting time, I was determined to be 100% responsible for all childcare costs including vacations, minus his two weeks during the summer.

Let us scream together for a moment... CHOOSE TO WORK? As if his desire to work was not an option but somehow, I, a career woman, had a choice to work or not work and would be punished with extended costs and limited time with my daughter should I choose to have a career!?! I felt defeated and deflated. Multiple attempts to reverse – even to the level of the Supreme Court on the financial portion – *failed.* I found myself frustrated and overwhelmed.

After sulking for a long while, I finally decided that the unfair confines of conventional thinking would not derail me. I would find a way to pursue my career aspirations and be a phenomenal mom to my two girls. With lots of testing, crying, and almost giving up multiple times, I finally started finding solutions. Those solutions started with me knocking down my self-imposed walls of broken confidence, beginning to dream big, and seeking support to guide me into waters untraveled. I am not saying that this was easy. There were many layers in my own self-image that had to be peeled back and built up. But it began with a decision to try.

I understand confidence flat-lining. I know how thoughts can create truths, albeit distorted ones. I invested in building my confidence – building the real me - over the next several years. It took a ton of effort and guidance (which is what this book and our programs are built upon), and thankfully my world looks very different now.

Now I run a six-figure leadership and wellness coaching business that makes my heart absolutely *sing!* We grow leadership in career with *leadership of self* as a top priority for hundreds of men and women in law enforcement, unveiling the fears and masks, and leading ourselves to excellence in both career and in our personal lives. I align myself with incredible professionals who find solutions, too, even when life is unfair – perceived or actual. I am proud that I can gift my daughters the best schools and opportunities that align with our family's core values. I am thankful that I was surrounded by people and coaches who helped me think out of the box in terms of *leadership of life* once I was open to those ideas, and I continue to surround myself with such gems. I am forever thankful that I have built my life by design! My life is filled with self-love, career excellence, and a mission to help others reach their highest potential with respect, excellence, and joy. It was an unbelievable journey; I learned clear action steps that all can take to rise above a lack of confidence much more quickly than I did.

Your Best Outcome

Module 5 is crucial for creating a life that energizes you, integrates work and home in harmony, and affords a sustainable career in law enforcement analytics. In our programs, I share exactly how I rose from a state of guilt and low confidence to now flourishing with *leadership of self,* a career that I love, financial stability, and incredible pride in the fantastic parent that I am! Our team delivers the roadmap to success every day to analysts and supervisors all over the world.

This module outlines tools to become confident and deeply valued leaders who thrive while achieving work-life harmony. We will work to uncover your fears, build your confidence, explore what environments and experiences bring your best self to the table, and develop an action plan to create sustainability in your work and personal life. It is possible to rise to be your best self and have a successful career in analytics and a life you love! I did, and so can you.

Smart Strategy

Since 2011, I have taught all over the country, and virtually throughout the world, for multiple government and regional entities. I have led instruction in everything from international three-month courses on building analytical capacity for supervisors to computer applications, tactical analysis, data analytics fundamentals, analytical best practices, data-driven strategy implementation, wellness in policing, and all that lies in between. I have worked with hundreds of junior and senior analysts and managers through one-on-one technical assistance, site visits, and frantic phone calls asking for help with managing, building, hiring, and getting analysts skilled in technical skills, mindset, and infrastructure.

Before that, from 1998 to 2011, I was an analyst and faced my challenges, delivered regional technical presentations, and fielded calls from analyst after analyst, all seeking the same thing. I can tell you that the number one challenge analysts and managers face is having *confidence!*

Chiefs ask me to help build their analysts' *confidence* so that they can take ownership of their roles, deliver what needs delivering without constant reassurance, and create impact through their expertise. Chiefs say (and I have personally observed) that often analysts depend on external validation; they thrive on praise and self-destruct if they perceive criticism. We have also talked about this theme repeatedly in our private, free Facebook group that delivers weekly live content to analysts and supervisors around the globe. (Visit us at Tribe of Excellence, https://bit.ly/3ikopiJ a community of service-based and emergency response professionals who work to create the social impact they desire while living their best lives!*)* Not owning your worth regardless of anyone else's opinion is a real issue that debilitates so many beautiful and worthy professionals.

Whether it's because you haven't truly fallen in love with yourself and the life you live or you're looking for approval through feedback from others, 90% of analysts and supervisors I know suffer deeply from a lack of confidence. They are regularly trying to "prove" that they and their work have value to the agency. Know that if you experience feelings of being 'less than' you are not alone. I, too, felt that way when I wore my mask. But feeling the need to be validated by external sources will be your downfall and lead you to experience a career that is overworking you, overwhelming you, and undervaluing you. The neediness blurs your boundaries. The lack of confidence deprives you of beautiful opportunities to give your gifts and create the impact available to you ... to live a fulfilled, joyous life with both career excellence and home excellence. I beg you, *build your confidence!* This chapter will show you how to begin to do so.

Inventory

Let's start with taking inventory of where you are. On a scale of one to ten, how do you feel about each of the following statements?

- I know my why/my purpose.
- I know my natural-given skills and talents.
- I understand the different analytical skills necessary for effective analytics.

- I understand the different technical skills necessary for effective analytics.
- I am building a blueprint/roadmap/plan to reach my technology and analytical skills necessary for effective analytics.
- I know the importance of partnerships and influence efforts in bringing faster results.
- I am aligned with partnership and influence efforts that will bring me faster results.
- I understand efficiency and synergy techniques that will close my productivity gap.
- I feel confident.
- I feel empowered.
- I feel like I am creating an unwavering belief in myself.
- I feel like I am growing a solid foundation in analytics fast and with focused resources.
- I feel like I am creating work-life harmony.
- I feel like I am creating great impact in law enforcement.
- I feel like I can reach my goals fast and with confidence and ease.
- I feel like I am highly effective, productive, and balanced.
- I feel like I am valued.
- I am working smarter, not harder.

Confidence Is A Skill

There are many exercises, TED Talks, motivational speeches, and resources to build confidence. But what works?

Confidence is a mental state that you can strengthen or diminish. It sets up a vibration that causes you and others to trust your ability, and thus increases your influence. But sometimes our confidence is shaken. I've talked with analysts who aren't sure if their products are any good, who believe they aren't good enough, who struggle to speak up and feel confident with the work they do. I want to hold them and encourage them, drilling into their heads that they *are* of value, that they *are* good enough! But confidence is an inside game.

So why is our confidence low? There are many reasons why we lack confidence – genes and temperament, life experiences, trauma, parenting styles we experienced as a child, neglect, abuse, appearance, gender, race, and sexual orientation challenges, misinformation, anxiety, depression, and more. Sometimes we can be ultra-confident, and a month later, our confidence dives. It's important to know that this is natural, temporary, and must be addressed to find joy, fulfillment, and career success.

Building your confidence is an essential step in creating harmony in your life, and it makes you a better analyst! It starts with the story you tell yourself. Your goal is to know your true, authentic self, and fall absolutely in love with you! You've got this!

Here are six strategies that will build your confidence.

1. Discover The Real You!

What skills and talents do you like about yourself the most? List as many as you can. Then list more! When are you the proudest? Most confident? The first step is giving attention to our talents and skills and reminding ourselves of those things at which we *do* excel! Having a positive self-image of ourselves encourages others to have a positive image of us. We must put out a positive vibration of thoughts of ourselves and our self-image. Some people refer to it as posture. We dive into these concepts a ton in our program through group coaching, personal coaching, and various special events that help us discover our true selves and enjoy the exploration! We learn how to pay attention to what makes us feel confident and intentionally search for those confidence-boosting opportunities.

2. Find Your Community

One of the challenges I hear from analysts all the time is that they are lonely. They work exhaustively, weakening their connection to a community they once loved. Work may feel safe, an area in which they feel in control, if there are struggles in other areas of their lives. It initiates a cycle in which they pour more into their work to feel successful. Before long, however, no one is calling them on a Friday night to hang out. They realize that their immediate circle of friends or family has shriveled or disappeared. They feel increasingly isolated and alone. They rely on work to be their all, the place they feel valued and joyful. When work becomes a challenge, however, there is nowhere for them to find an escape. They are stuck and continue the cycle of overwhelm and loneliness.

Connection to a strong community is invigorating and empowering. Connection to a community builds confidence and resilience in such a fantastic way. Imagine saying this statement six months from now:

"I am so thankful that my relationships have deepened with friends and mentors. I have the most authentic, kind, sincere, loyal, and committed individuals in my life! They are so dear to me, and we help each other grow on so many levels. We are each other's major support systems. We nurture our future successes. They are brilliant in areas where I am still growing. They inspire me, stretch me, and call me to my greatness! They pour light into me, and I pour light into them. We share knowledge, amplify each other's lives, and bring each other greater prosperity. I am aligned with, and supported by, top achievers and other persons of consequence, surrounded by rocket boosters, leaders, and catalysts of positive change. We meet weekly for lunch or another activity and attend annual retreats together. I am so deeply connected and know I will never feel alone again!"

I encourage you to find your community – reach out to friends, spiritual communities, online groups with similar interests, book clubs – and develop meaningful connections with them. This may be challenging at first, but you and they deserve a beautiful relationship! Building your community creates success and connection and brings a marvelous sense of belonging, thus increasing your confidence.

Many analysts in our private program meet every week as a cohesive unit, supporting and growing together. Some connect privately for deeper connections and support. We have special monthly events relative to *leadership of self* (which we will discuss in detail soon) that further bond these analysts for life.

We regularly raise each other as we "Pop the Champagne" and celebrate each other's successes, big and small, career and home-related, together. We are a community. We are an RG Family.

3. Finding The Good In Others

The third step to building confidence is to find the good in others. Look for what others do well and let them know that you have noticed this about them. Give them a sincere compliment. Notice that we began to work on this in Module 3: Partnerships and Influence. Being authentic and helping others see the good in themselves will reflect on the goodness inside of ourselves. Try this; for the next seven days, find the goodness in three different people a day. Tell them. See how it shifts your life and theirs!

4. Developing Your Strengths

We have already begun to do this as we have written out our macro and micro goals in each of the core competency areas relative to being an analyst. Continuing to strengthen our skill sets will give us the courage to tell ourselves, "I know I am good and understand why I am good." That is confidence! Have you built your professional development roadmap yet? Have you based your roadmap on the skills you want to master (not the classes you want to take)? Have you decided what you will excel in and started tackling it? Consider mastering one or two of your strengths and then teaching them to other analysts, perhaps at a local analyst networking session. You will build your community and your confidence.

5. *Build A Portfolio*

Analysts must consider an action plan to build their confidence, both for the analyst and the agency. Analysts can share success stories, highlight what is working, and provide growth opportunities. One excellent way to create confidence (and buy-in!) is for the analyst to build a portfolio of work products (with permission and redacted, of course!) These portfolios help the agency understand the analyst's role, skills, and talents and articulate how others can utilize the function correctly. These can also be used as reminders to the analysts of their quality contribution to the agency's overall goals.

Here is how to create a portfolio:

- Use a binder to store the components of the portfolio. Create sections relative to work experience. For example, add a section on tactical projects, strategic analysis, annual reports, etc. Remember to focus on *successes* and how your *analysis* created an impact! Articulate it!
- Add a work product to each section - a sentence or paragraph regarding what the analysis included and who utilized it (i.e., detectives, patrol.)
- Document stories of what the analyst did and how it created impact (e.g. - arrest made.)
- Include a section for certifications, training, and other professional development.
- Encourage the analyst to add new products as they advance in skills. This can also highlight officers who effectively utilized the analytical function, thus promoting additional feedback and buy-in.

6. *Create Quality Boundaries And Stick To Them!*

You are the CEO, not only of Crime Analysis but of your life. So, if you want boundaries to be in place, you've got to be the one to make them. One of the biggest problems I often see when analysts try to set boundaries is that they don't share them with other people.

The primary thing you can do right now to make your boundaries more successful is to establish a support system. Who's in your support system? Who do you run ideas past? Who helps you hold your boundaries? Are you strong in your church? Do you have a coach or friend group? I'm not talking about your family; sometimes they're the ones you need to hold boundaries with. If you're anything like me, you've always been the rock, the strong one, and it's been a challenge to ask for help. I've recognized in my life that to move forward, I need a support system to bounce ideas off and to hold me accountable.

The second thing you can do is allow other people to be angry when you set boundaries. When you begin to set boundaries that others may not like, they might not understand, and that's okay. It's vital that you do not change your "No." For instance, you aren't available to work weekends, but your boss says they need you on-call 24/7. You can say, "We need to come up with another solution." You can be open to other solutions, but don't make a habit of setting aside your boundaries.

Be prepared to distance yourself from someone with whom you are trying to set boundaries. These are people who may make you weaken the boundaries you're trying so hard to create.

Bonus Tip

September 20, 2021 was the very first "National Crime and Intelligence Analyst Appreciation Day"! The NCIAA Day highlights the dedicated work performed by law enforcement and military analysts behind the scenes. As you know, these professionals give their gifts, time, and energy to help officers and detectives work smarter, not harder, analyzing criminal enterprises, identifying homicide suspects, and everything in between. This day is to say *thank you* for everything the analytical community does every single day. If you are an analyst, celebrate *you* and your contribution to the law enforcement community. Don't be shy. Stick a poster on your door, take yourself out to dinner or for a walk, celebrate the wonderful work you do! If you know an analyst, reach out to them, and celebrate them! This will build confidence, community, and your relationships.

Although this chapter is all about confidence, know that you have been building your confidence since page one of this book! In creating clarity relative to where you want your life to go, being a *leader of self,* and growing your skills and competencies, you are developing a more significant impact in law enforcement. You are creating a solid foundation in analytics. And you are doing all of this while learning to maintain a deep commitment to personal leadership and fulfillment. I'm so proud of you and the work that you are doing for yourself. I can tell that you are starting to see fundamental changes happening in your life.

This is just the beginning! Congratulations on taking life-changing steps toward becoming a leader in law enforcement analytics and realizing your life by design.

Success Highlights

Alex L. is a law enforcement professional who started in our RG coaching programs in March 2020. Since then, she has participated in 9 of our programs - learning, growing, and evolving! Recently, she was promoted to Police Planner, a coveted position responsible for performing complex, statistical, and analytical research work and supervising operations. Here is her story of resilience: https://bit.ly/2ZwVxNF

Jenna B. has one of my favorite analyst success stories! She was in our RG Program for three rounds, joining to improve her self-confidence, work productivity, and create better work-life harmony. It took her engine a little while to get heated, but she was on fire once it did! She went from not taking care of herself at all, couldn't even look in the mirror, to taking excellent care of herself with monthly visits to the sauna, chiropractor, acupuncture, reducing her chips and candy consumption at night by over 50%, developing systems at work that improved data quality and analytics, and finding her friends and joy for life again. She finally started knowing that she is worth her best living. Jenna also found her relationship with her son again, inspiring him to eat well, enjoy life, and build positive connections. Her life is *entirely* different now and filled with excellence in her career and love for her home life. So proud of you, Jenna!

Laura C. has seen incredible growth in just three months of being in our programs! Laura had struggled with confidence and guilt for quite some time (heck, a ton of us do!) when she finally decided to create change in her life. Three months ago, she committed to round two wellness coaching with our team -

broken, disheartened, but hopeful and committed to change. She was struggling with communicating with ease at work, connecting with her family, and working through the responsibilities of organizing her mother's estate.

Week after week, she showed up gaining more and more clarity about her goals. She was vulnerable and committed to making change. There were uncomfortable tears and stretching in a way she was not able to do on her own. Each session, she "showed up" with excellence. She executed success list after success list. I was so proud of her for her commitment to the process.

After three months, Laura is finally coming above water. She has found absolute joy, pride, and love of herself, again. She has found her voice with her managers, has fallen back in love with herself, has made deep connections to family and friends, and now takes excellent care of herself. Notably, she shared, "I would never have gotten to where I am without listening to you, even when I thought you were crazy. I did not think the program was going to fix me. But it worked!! I showed up, did the work, & listened. I am taking better care of myself. I am proud of the work that I did with my mom's estate planning. My mom knew that she was loved and that it was okay to go and be with dad. Thanks for guiding me toward living my best life."

Inspired Action Exercise

Building Confidence

Reflect on the following questions and create inspired action to take this week:

1. On a scale of one to ten, how strong is my confidence? What is the root of my score?
2. What do I like most about myself? Read the answers every evening before you go to bed.
3. What top three skills am I working to develop? Strengthening my skills will bring me confidence! Knowledge is power.
4. What good can I see in others? When will I tell them?
5. What negative talk is taking real estate in my brain? What am I willing to let go of? What language will I use to replace it?
6. Recite the mantras (see your free gift below) every day for sixty-six days. See how your paradigms shift!

Now, read the statement below and finish it with an empowering affirmation. Create a list of at least ten affirmations like those in the examples below:

I am so happy and grateful now that...

1. I am growing my confidence. I feel empowered.
2. I am proud of my quality work.
3. I grow a solid foundation in analytics/crime analysis faster and with focused resources.
4. I create work-life harmony.
5. I am creating a greater impact in law enforcement.

6. I maximize my resources and create efficiencies.
7. I create excellent personal leadership and fulfillment.
8. I have an unwavering belief in myself.
9. I am reaching my goals faster and with confidence and ease.
10. I am transforming my quality of life and work by becoming highly effective, productive, and balanced.
11. I am maintaining excellent personal balance.
12. I am becoming super confident in my analytical work.
13. I am becoming an industry leader and am valued deeply.
14. I work smarter, not harder.

Analyst Mantras

Thinking yourself into success!

My gift to you: Analyst Mantras

> *I am really struggling with work-life harmony. Where do I begin?*

Try these Analyst Mantras (https://bit.ly/3F1Insq) on for size. See how they create a more quality day.

MODULE 6
STEP INTO LEADERSHIP
THINK LIKE A LEADER

> *"Dawn's drive is to help us create a healthy professional and personal life balance, to encourage us to be the leaders we have the capacity to be in our agencies. Repeat to yourself...I'm the CEO of Crime Analysis...it'll be easier to do Leadership of Self."*
> — RHEA GERSTENKORN

Why This Matters

One of my favorite books of all time, *Think and Grow Rich* by Napoleon Hill, has genuinely impacted the way I live my life by design and has led me on a path to thinking myself into results. Hill contends that everything happens twice, once in our minds and then in reality. He provides specific theories and steps to develop and achieve our desired goals. Reading his book multiple times and applying his ideas initiated my awareness of the role that thinking plays in my riches. I began to create thoughts, have faith, and develop a single-minded plan to create outcomes I desired intensely. Those results included running my own successful business with ease and flow and creating large-scale community impact.

His teachings soon led me to the studies of other thought leaders like Tony Robbins, Joe Dispenza, Dale Carnegie, Bob Proctor, Lisa Nichols, and others. I have learned from years of study and application that to break out of old patterns, we must raise our level of *awareness.* To think like a leader and understand and serve others, we must first become aware of and understand ourselves. Understanding involves conversations we have with ourselves that lead us to positive outcomes.

As a graduate of the "Thinking into Results" program for leaders by the Proctor Gallagher Institute, and a student of the beautiful notion that we can engineer our lives by design, I deeply understand and value the role that thoughts and core belief systems play in our success. And how once we become intently aware of both, we can make daily decisions that align with our thoughts and beliefs with ease.

I spent a lot of time thinking and dreaming about what I wanted to be true in my life. I explored and defined what I wanted in my family relationships, my friend relationships, my love relationship, my income and business revenue, my investments and future legacy, my philanthropic endeavors, my business design, and what I wanted my home, my vacations, and my days to look and feel like. I identified my fears and released them one by one.

I became ultra-clear on my desires and developed an inspired action plan to achieve them. It works. All I set out to do has been accomplished or is in process. This is true for our clients as well. We have interwoven these concepts into the threads of our programs and have seen success after success with its application. As you can imagine, this involves deep exploration guided by our coaches. I'd like to share some fundamental leadership concepts with you that can get you started on your journey even before you begin working with a coach.

Your Best Outcome

This module is all about *thinking like a leader.* Feeling like a leader is a crucial success factor in becoming a sought-after professional in the law enforcement analytical field. Practicing leadership skills will accelerate creating massive movement and success for yourself and for those you help to elevate! This chapter involves the conversations you have with yourself that lead to positive outcomes. Focus areas include thinking and mindset, creating a higher vibration, and rising to the challenge of leading others.

Smart Strategy

If you are regularly talking negatively or accepting when others do so, then you are *thinking* negatively. And when you *think* negatively, this impacts your subconscious mind, and your feelings and actions will be negative. Your paradigm, or the multitude of habits, will continue to keep you in the cycle of negativity. You must go to the root – or the subconscious programming – to shift the paradigm and create new, healthier habits. To move to higher productivity and greater rewards, you must intentionally reprogram your mind. Let's try a real-life example, OK?

You have no idea if your bulletins are being used for good. Can you relate? Your thought process might be, "I stink. I haven't had enough training. No one even cares what I do in Crime Analysis. *I* don't even *know* what I do in Crime Analysis! The officers are lazy. They don't want to be proactive. Creating bulletins is useless." Or... your thought process might be different.

"Hmmm... I wonder if my bulletins are effective. The work that I produce is quality and on point. I'm always on time, and the bulletins contain actionable analyses to help our officers and detectives. Let me brainstorm some ideas of how to get it into hands that will use this information to police smarter."

When we shift our mindset and create effective habits and strategies in our own lives, we create *simple excellence* that best serves our police departments *and* ourselves. It's essential to recognize that practicing leadership skills will move you toward creating massive forward movement and success!

There are several fundamental elements of the CEO mindset that have truly impacted my career and personal life. When you consciously begin to think like a leader or CEO, by shifting your mindset and creating effective habits and strategies, you increase your efficiency and effectiveness and improve outcomes for yourself and everyone around you. First, improve your thoughts and mindset. Then, think like a CEO of Crime Analysis. Next, create a higher vibration of you. Finally, lead others!

1. Improve Your Thoughts And Mindset

Do you get caught up in hurtful self-talk?

"There's nothing I can do to make a change. This is just the way it is. I'm too old/comfortable to make waves. Life sucks. Get used to it. I do everything around here. I'm just not smart enough. I don't have enough experience. I only have eight years left for retirement and then I'll find something better. They expect me to do everything. My boss is a micromanager. Our new Chief won't let me do anything..." Yadda, yadda, yadda!

Do any of these sound like the conversations that *you* have with yourself or with your family or co-workers - sometimes or most of the time? Do you find yourself singing a symphony of negativity and "stuckness"? Be honest!

What story are you telling yourself each day? Do you have a fixed mindset? Are the thoughts that fill your head negative? Do you allow your fears, lack of confidence, and negative self-talk to keep you in negativity? Do you believe your basic abilities, intelligence, and talents are fixed traits? That there's nothing you can do about them?

Or do you have a growth mindset – you see the opportunities and potential around you?

2. Think Like A CEO of Crime Analysis

Analysts must consider themselves the CEO of Crime Analysis - and honestly, the CEO of their lives! When you are a CEO, you think with a strategic vision (setting the overall direction of the unit.) You spearhead growth initiatives that support providing exceptional value for strategy development, create alliances with internal and external partners for win-win

107

relationships, construct opportunities for optimized results, and generate efficiencies and systems that ensure flow and improvement paths. You think *big picture.* You identify the gaps and close them.

We have an entire program dedicated to leadership development. In this book we start with the basics; thinking yourself into leadership. Recite to yourself, "I am the CEO of Crime Analysis. I am the CEO of my life!"

3. Create A Higher Vibration Of You

Much research (from Tony Robbins, Lewis Howes, Chris Hogan's *Everyday Millionaire,* and others) points to *gratitude* as the number one awareness builder, happiness builder, and even wealth builder!

A recent study found that gratitude (*Happier Human)* impacts us in the following 25 ways:

1. Makes us happier
2. Makes people like us - Gratitude makes us nicer, more trusting, more social, and more appreciative. As a result, it helps us make more friends, deepens our existing relationships, and improves our marriage
3. Makes us healthier and extends our lives by a few months or years
4. Strengthens our emotions - Gratitude reduces feelings of envy, makes our memories happier, lets us experience good feelings, and helps us bounce back from stress
5. Develops our personality
6. Makes us more optimistic

7. Reduces materialism - Materialism is strongly correlated with reduced well-being and increased rates of mental disorders

8. Increases spiritualism

9. Makes us less self-centered

10. Increases self-esteem

11. Improves our sleep - Gratitude increases sleep quality, reduces the time required to fall asleep, and increases sleep duration. Said differently, gratitude can reduce insomnia

12. Keeps you away from the doctor – 137 research studies indicate that positive emotion improves health. The details are complicated, but the overall picture is not – if you want to improve your health, improve your mind

13. Increases our energy

14. Makes us more likely to exercise

15. Helps us bounce back

16. Makes us feel good

17. Reduces envy

18. Helps us relax

19. Deepens friendships

20. Makes us more effective leaders

21. Specifically, multiple studies have found expressions of gratitude to be highly motivating, while expressions of criticism are slightly de-motivating

22. Helps us network

23. Improves goal achieving

24. Improves decision making

25. Increases productivity - As gratitude has been shown to increase self-esteem and reduce insecurity, it can help us focus and improve our productivity

Get gratitude into your day *every day* to become a much better version of yourself!

To increase your gratitude, do some or all of the following:

- Keep a gratitude journal.
- Write or think of three things daily that you're thankful for.
- Reflect gratefully before decision making.
- Meditate.
- Read *Millionaire Mindset* by Lewis Howes.
- Practice rest and recovery.
- Find stillness and listen.
- Use mantras.

4. Lead Others

Much has been written about leadership across industries and time. Are you a born leader? Or can you learn to lead? It is understood that leadership differs from management, and most agree leadership can be taught and therefore learned. There are certain qualities every leader shares, however. These traits include self-discipline, a focus on the end result, an insatiable appetite for knowledge with an equal ability to implement quickly, humility coupled with conviction, a readiness to see the light in others, a willingness to forge ahead - to blaze the trail - while reaching back to help others follow, and an authentic desire to add value driven by the question, "How can I serve?"

Learning to lead others requires you to learn to lead yourself first. To do that, you must be aware it's possible and then you must decide it's something you aspire to do; become a leader and lead. It sounds obvious yet it involves a conscious decision.

Awareness and industry leadership involve the conversations you have with yourself that lead you to positive outcomes. Practicing leadership thinking and gratitude while elevating others allows you to create massive movement and success! Being a leader in the industry takes time and concentrated effort. Listening to leadership podcasts, reading books on leadership, attending leadership events, and working one-on-one with a mentor can genuinely impact your progression as an industry leader.

In our RG and RG Leadership Programs, we spend quite a bit of time walking through exactly what it takes to think and act like a leader. Whether or not you hold the title, you must understand that you *are* the CEO of Crime Analysis and the CEO of *your life*! Remember the discussion of Napoleon Hill that began this chapter? Analysts must design their lives first in their minds and then in reality. When we start with a desire, we can engineer the makings of that desire in reverse.

We'd love to help you *find your genius* and help you build a *desire* for life/work harmony filled with purpose and leadership thinking. We can provide tools and help you uncover the energy you need to succeed! Together, we will continue to shift the law enforcement culture so you may achieve an excellent career growth path alongside self-leadership! You are ready. You are equipped. You are empowered. Genius is yours; now go *get it*!

Success Highlights

Jessica Y. is a long-time analyst supervisor who was searching for tools to build her analytical infrastructure within her agency as well as her own leadership. After only a couple months in the program, she built out analytical systems, her core leadership characteristics, and created a stronger work-life harmony. Go Jessica!

She shares, "This Leadership Incubator has in a sense given me the support I was looking for to work on creating the best version of myself. This is done with such honesty and thoughtfulness that it is impossible not to be moved to change. I am enormously grateful for the forces at work that led me to this leadership group, and I look forward to working and growing my leadership skills. I am finding myself being more intentional and long for meaningful change - inspiring me to join Facebook, just to have access to the Tribe, is nothing short of a small miracle."

Inspired Action Exercise

Answer the following questions:

1. Do you get caught up in unfavorable self-talk?
2. What do you want your life to look like?
3. Recite to yourself, "I am the CEO of Crime Analysis. I am the CEO of my life!"
4. What are three inspired action steps you can take to create a higher vibration of yourself?
5. How can you be a leader to others today?

6. On this scale of one to ten, rate your current level of influence and where you want to be in terms of impact and buy-in at your agency.

7. What holds you back from exercising leadership, whether or not you have the title?

Excellence in Analytics

My gift to you: Creating Buy-In & Influence

> *How do you create buy-in relative to the proper use of analytics at your agency?*

Leadership thinking involves creating a data-driven culture and buy-in within agencies and must be a focused effort. First, analysts must be deliberate, purposeful, and positioned as an authority to gain influence and respect as an integral component of the agency's strategic operations. Second, creating buy-in and influence must be intentional and persistent agency-wide, and must include building and nurturing internal relationships. Strategies that agencies can implement today will lead to greater influence and buy-in, flowing feedback loops, and a stronger and fully integrated data-driven function. In the end, buy-in and influence strengthen the utility of the agency's desired analytical results and provide opportunities for officers to succeed. Check out this free audio and download <u>Creating Buy-In and Influence</u> (<u>https://bit.ly/3F4QvZe</u>) to learn ten tips to create influence at your agency.

MODULE 7
LEADERSHIP OF SELF

> *"Leadership of self is just as important as the work we do!"*
> — ALI LEDUC

Why This Matters

Leadership of self is the key component to professional and personal growth and happiness. Over the last ten years, I spent many waking hours learning to perform service with excellence while discovering my unique path to happiness. I read numerous self-help books, listened to endless podcasts and training programs around self-care, and worked with many expert coaches to help me gain clarity and release guilt around my personal wellness goals. Through these paths, I identified obstacles and fears that I faced in achieving them. My coaches could see things I simply could not see with my then-current lenses. I challenged my fears, took inspired action, and sought accountability to reach my desired health and wellness and career outcomes. I overcame perfectionism, revealing my dark secrets, and thriving in doing so! And it all started with shifting my paradigm... shifting my belief to include *leadership of self* as the top priority.

Now I want to help you, and I don't want it to take you ten years! I want every supervisor and analyst struggling to balance excellent service with joy to learn what is needed to live a life of fulfillment and purpose. We built our entire business around this concept. We focus intensely on the fact that you can have this fantastic, excellent, organized, professional career in alignment with a life that brings you fulfillment, joy, happiness, and wellness. All our programs and tools (including this book!) involve *leadership of self* as a top priority, as the propeller that ignites all other genius in your life. Throughout these modules, I hope you have started to understand and desire a new way. I found the best version of me, and so can you!

Your Best Outcome

The most critical step in all our training is to lead with self-love and self-care first; *leadership of self* must be a priority. Becoming your best self involves optimizing multiple areas in your life. It means that you finally are ready to receive the best in others and the best that your life has waiting for you. When you fuel your body, spirit, and mind with excellence, you can create a life that you love to live and provide the highest quality of service to your team and your community. You find joy and deep fulfillment in so many aspects of your life!

Smart Strategy

Leadership of Self; this is an area where analysts often pay little to no attention. We all have priorities – work, family, kids, parents, side hustles. We often put ourselves last on the list. We tell ourselves that our wants and desires are last; that we can push and push ourselves to the limit. Check out the list below. Do any of these sound familiar to you?

1. I don't leave my desk for lunch.
2. I sit for more than one hour at a time.
3. I respond to emails/texts before or after work hours.
4. I have a goal to work out, but I'm so tired I just can't get out of bed in the morning, or I just don't have time to go to the gym after work.
5. I haven't had a facial in a few months or ever!
6. My "me time" consists of passing out at night.
7. I constantly get sick.
8. I feel run down.
9. My "to-do list" is never-ending.
10. I have a hard time relaxing. I can't sleep at night.
11. I feel overwhelmed.
12. I can't remember the last time I did X for me.

If you are nodding your head vigorously right now, feeling like this is you, listen on. We have solutions! You can live a life you love, even if you don't quite yet know how to do so. This book, our Tribe of Excellence community, and our programs pave the path for you. You just need to *desire* a better way.

In yoga, there are concepts of Strength and Ease. To perform the perfect pose, there must be a combination of strength and ease to sustain the pose. For instance, there's a pose called Tree Pose where you stand on one leg, and your hands either come to your heart or branch out like trees. You must have equal amounts of strength and ease; Strength in your foundation, your legs, and core, all the while your face is soft, and your breath is calm.

If you ever see someone doing a tree pose, you will notice that her hips point forward, her hands are at her heart center, her shoulders are back away from her ears, and her chest is lifted; t*his is alignment.* Also, notice that all four corners of her planted foot are rooted into the earth, that her thigh is engaged, that her knee is actively pushing outward. *This is strength.* Finally, notice that her gaze is forward, her foot is on her thigh, not pushing into her knee, and there is a smile on her face; *this is awareness.* It is only when strength and ease are in equal parts that we can truly succeed. And how we get there is through mindset, routines, and habits.

Analysts need to understand and align with a purpose (why we are in the field to begin with) and our unique ability (what we are good at.) *This is alignment.* We need to create systems and assessments and build our skills, roll up our sleeves, and push when needed, temporarily. *This is strength.* We need to face our fears and self-doubt while building our confidence and personal value. We need to lead with a commitment to treating ourselves impeccably and directing our lives with ourselves as a priority. *This is awareness.* It is only when strength and ease are in equal parts that we truly succeed. And how we get there is through our mindsets, building quality relationships and influence, implementing productivity habits, and committing to continuous growth. These are our mindsets, routines, and practices. Can you see how this is all tying together?

Restoration versus Recovery

My "*me time*" used to be plopping in front of the TV after a long day and binging on Law and Order or Chicago PD TV. I was so exhausted after my day in law enforcement analytics that I just wanted to be mindless... and brainless TV or passing out early were my go-to's. Can you relate? Are you sick of thinking, "I am too busy" or "I am too tired?" Is brainless TV or that second glass of wine your go-to?

What I learned is that this kind of passive recovery isn't recovery at all. Yes, it's enjoyable sometimes, but it didn't restore me in a way that made me *operate at a higher level*. It only perpetuated the cycle of working hard with no energy return and little joy. Suppose you want to get sciency about it (like I did as an Institute of Integrative Nutrition graduate; December 2021.) In that case, the "work, work, work" mentality jacks up your cortisol levels, puts pressure on your adrenals, hinders your immune system, and wreaks havoc on your digestive system... not to mention the relentless added weight gain to those hips and thighs!

If you want to build boundaries and habits that help align your career with wellness priorities, *you can*! I've learned that it takes active recovery to perform service with excellence while discovering your path to happiness. Active recovery makes you more productive and happier! Active recovery restores what has been depleted, revitalizes what has been used up, and brings us the energy and creativity to fulfill our work missions with precision and ease.

So how do we build in active recovery?

I do a lot of traveling, guest speaking at conferences, events, and other speaking engagements, delivering hands-on instruction, and speaking on podcasts and other platforms. The other day, my co-worker, Caroline, and I had a great time with the New Hampshire Association of Chiefs of Police at their annual trade show discussing effective deployment and wellness strategies for emergency response professionals. I *love* the energy and thrill that inspiring others brings to me. On a personal level, it truly makes my heart sing! But teaching, training, and engaging takes a ton out of me. I always - *must* - build in recovery to achieve my highest performance and long-term, sustainable success. My recovery is relatively simple but gets the job done. Here is a three-minute video (https://bit.ly/3F4QvZe) on what that recovery looked like for me after the trade show! (Must be a member of our Tribe of Excellence Facebook community to view the video; we can't wait for you to join!)

The same might be true for you. You may not be a public speaker, but you work hard and have a ton of responsibilities. Do you want to build ease into your day? Feel fulfilled while replenishing your spirit and energy so that you can give more and enjoy life outside of work? Here are a few recovery ideas for you to try:

- Stimulate the vagus nerve by taking breathing breaks.
- Do yoga, meditation, tai chi, qigong, biofeedback, and play music.
- Go outside.
- Move your body.
- Fuel your body with whole foods and less inflammatory foods such as refined sugars.

- Use heat therapy such as an ultra-detox bath or a sauna.
- Connect with friends!
- Try herbs such as Ginseng, Ashwagandha, or Rhodiola Rosea.
- Seek out stress-busting tools such as GPS for the Soul or apps on your iPhone.

Whatever recovery method you choose, build recovery as a key component to your successful and joyous life! If you need some support, we have a ton of resources for you! Check us out at https://dawnreeby.podia.com/

Remember, you are the CEO of your life. The design of your life is how you decided it will be! You have the power to determine the life you want to live!

Three Steps To Owning Your Day

Let's discuss the concept of "owning your day." There are three steps to owning your day and owning your time. It's all about personal leadership and how to make it so that you are leading precisely the life that you want to lead.

Sometimes we don't necessarily say 'no' to the things we should. We may take on an extra assignment, or perhaps we volunteer when we don't want to do so. Perhaps we get on the phone with someone who's going to drain us of positive energy, right? You know what I'm talking about. You know the things that you say yes to that you don't want to. I'm here to help you earn back that time and establish *leadership of self.* Let's explore three essential tips for personal leadership.

Step 1

The first step in this three-part process is to *define what your priorities are in the first place.* My number one priority is my health. I must eat the right foods and surround myself with people who will be healthy for me. Supporting myself physically and emotionally with all that fun stuff is priority number one to get to the other two. My children are my second priority; my two girls.... family. I love my babies, and they are a priority for me. My third priority is building my business, helping to support the law enforcement community and helping them find that wellness and genius they deserve.

So, what is important to you? What is important to you in your work environment? What is important to you in your home environment? Think about this; instead of being reactive to what comes your way, I encourage you to be a bit more proactive. Sit down and think about what is important to you. What are your top three non-negotiables? Defining your top priorities is step one because knowing your purpose and priorities help guide you to step two.

Step 2

Step two is *figuring out if other people or activities align with your priorities.* If you get a call during dinnertime with family, and family is a priority, that call interferes with a priority; it doesn't align. You're allowed to say, 'no.' Guiltlessly. You're allowed to say 'no' to the things that don't serve you. You are entitled to design your life in a way that benefits you, building in breaks, restoration, and enjoyment.

If you need a little boost with setting boundaries, check out these videos:

- 4-Part Boundaries Series: https://bit.ly/3ASCETa
- *Leadership of Self* & Guiltless Boundaries: https://bit.ly/3ogzmWv
- Keys to Setting Priorities: https://youtu.be/sxjpX-ylluQ

Step 3

Once you've identified and then determined what aligns and does not, you move onto step three, which is to *decline quickly and kindly*. Quickly - versus saying 'maybe later' - because it's not authentic if you know it doesn't align. It's not sincere to the person making the request. To be precise, be quick. And then the second part is to be kind and use good words. When other people's priorities don't align with yours, one thing you can say is, "This doesn't fit within my bandwidth now." Or you can say, "Hey, listen, I'm caught up right now. I'd love to learn or hear more about what you're saying. Let's talk tomorrow."

Being able to ask yourself, 'what are my priorities and does their request align with them' is a practical approach. And then tactfully, quickly, politely, and kindly saying 'no' when it doesn't serve you. *Those* are three steps to reclaim some time in your day, to feel guiltless about saying no to those things that don't align with your priorities. These three steps propel you towards *leadership of self*.

Various concepts and applications of *leadership of self* have been sprinkled throughout this book and all our programming, tools, and special events. *Leadership of Self* is the key to career and home victory. Be prepared to find a successful career filled with joy, fulfillment, and self-love because prioritizing you positions you to succeed on multiple levels. You become your best possible self. You lift others to become their best personal selves. You create solid boundaries, find growth in failure, and lean into the experiences and wonderful people the Universe has placed on your path. You are deserving. You are worthy. You are the CEO of your life. Lead your life by design. This is *leadership of self.*

Success Highlights

Andrew B. came to RG barely keeping his head above water from a challenging situation with his employer. He didn't feel valued at his agency yet he truly desired to be on a leadership path. He realized his foundation was missing and sought to create a more robust baseline to grow his career. He noted that his biggest challenge was believing in himself and finding his confidence.

Through his work in RG and two cycles in RG Leadership so far, Andrew has grown exponentially! He is now on the path to a supervisory position, backed with an incredible leadership foundation. With the guidance of his coach, he also found hidden talents relative to building quality relationships and intelligence analysis that he now teaches to others in our group, including instruction at the IACA Conference! He found a closer connection to his spirituality, deepened his goal setting with his partner in his personal life, and even started a legacy business making toxin-free candles. Andrew is now more positive, reflective, and intentional – not just in his work life but also in his home life! We are so incredibly proud of you, Andrew!

Inspired Action Exercise

Where do you go from here? Reflect on the steps below. Begin to create your blueprint – your life by design – with action steps to get there.

1. Start small – Take ten minutes to do a quick inventory of your relationships outside the workplace. Would your family, friends, and loved ones describe you as present? When was the last time you reached out to a friend just to catch up? When was the last time you did something just for yourself? If you're reading this and saying, "I'm too busy to do an inventory," then this message is especially for you. If you don't think you have 10 minutes to inventory, ask your loved ones if they feel you are present. Feeling shy about asking because you suspect you know the answer? Bingo! You just completed your inventory.

2. With the inventory completed, the next step is to do something else small. Leave at the end of your shift. If you work 8 am - 5 pm, *leave* at 5 pm. Don't tell yourself that you must stay to finish this one thing. The one thing will still be there tomorrow. If you're like me and you begin to feel guilty, tell others you have an appointment; you do... with yourself! These tiny steps are the beginning of taking your life back, and little by little, you will see the benefits. You will also find others will

become more respectful of your time as they learn you are not constantly available.

3. Take these small steps and set goals to take back your life. You deserve vacations, weekends, lunches, breaks that are work-worry-free. You deserve to give yourself the time you so freely give to others, to be fully present and enjoy your own life.

Power Planning Matrix

Analyst tool to track and manage goals.

My gift to you: Power Planning Matrix For Analysts

How do I improve my skills or know which skills to improve, while leading with self-care first?

A professional development roadmap based on the desired results relative to the analyst's vision, skills, talents, and passions must be established, prioritized, and revisited regularly. The road map should include relative training, quality networking, instructional efforts, building buy-in, leadership development, and other results-focused growth opportunities. Essentially, agencies must think with the end in mind when developing a roadmap to fill gaps, encourage learning, and promote ownership and growth. Our RG Program (https://bit.ly/3iiAbKJ)

completely assesses the skills of any analyst (crime, intelligence, etc.) and designs a progressive and customized plan with each client. You can also get started with this free Power Planning Matrix(https://bit.ly/3il0e3U) to create structure to your goals in each of the core focus areas key to industry success and work-life harmony.

PRELUDE
THE NEXT BOOK!

There is another book coming after *Bigger Than Data,* and it's about *Leadership.*

Law enforcement agencies often lack training and support for leaders. Although these leaders begin with good intentions, they soon feel burned out due to the following: a lack of confidence, being undertrained in leadership, having inefficient systems and processes, and feeling as if they are constantly spinning, overwhelmed, and stuck.

Whether you are currently in a supervisory role, rising to one, or simply wanting to be the leader of your own life, you are ready for hyper-growth. You want to build your leadership characteristics, create efficient and proactive systems, and develop a cohesive culture that promotes performance excellence! You want to make the social impact that you started to do while simultaneously leading a healthy life outside of the walls of service. You want to start taking good care of yourself finally! You want to reconnect with your family and friends and live a real life of happiness and joy. You are ready to become the leader that others are proud to follow, and you want to live a life filled with joy!

This (second) book and related leadership training are for professionals who want to build their leadership foundation, create efficient and proactive systems, and develop a cohesive culture that promotes performance excellence in the law enforcement analytical environment. It aids law enforcement agencies in effectively designing and implementing a long-term data-driven infrastructure that professionalizes analytical efforts and serves the agency and community exceptionally. The chapters provide various strategies, tools, and templates to build an agency's analytical capacity and legacy in a way that nurtures, grows, and retains quality analytical function and purpose. And because *leadership of self* is woven into the fabric of the book and coursework, supervisors will be sprinkled with concepts and tools to hold *leadership of self* as a priority. Combined, these solutions help leaders maintain a healthy life outside the walls of service and still make the social impact they are in leadership to accomplish.

Our team takes 40+ years of expertise in building government systems and strategies with the discipline of *leadership of self* as the top priority so that these public servants can achieve excellent careers while living the lives they love. We know what it takes to build your systems as we are one of the handful of entities that create nationally and internationally certified curriculum and deliver it globally! We are subject matter experts for multiple federal entities. We set the stage for establishing best practices in the industry relative to data-driven strategies in the public sector. And we have worked with hundreds of agencies in various capacities to help them design and implement successful, proactive strategies.

We also know what it is like to feel like unbalanced hamsters spinning in a sea of "to-do lists," experiencing adrenal fatigue, and suffering in our home lives. We have personally experienced what it takes to release the masks, regain our own lives, and become well-bodied professionals who love the lives we live. We found exactly what it takes to be efficient, effective, connected, confident, happy, and excellent! We sincerely believe that you can have it all - an outstanding career in service and an excellent home life by design. We are determined to show every service-based professional in the world how to live lives they absolutely love!

By the end of this second book, you will have a comprehensive understanding of the following: how to create a sustainable implementation plan for an analytical function inclusive of vision, policies and procedures, leadership and legacy strategies, results-focused thinking, and an assessment process that continues the unit's success far into the future.

Chapter 1 Sneak Peek - Creating a Vision:

The purpose of this chapter is to help you begin to create a vision of the analytical function. Upon doing so, it will guide all other lessons and applications. The vision describes the long-term desired results (one to three years into the future) and will be the compass that drives all efforts. When creating a vision, the agency must courageously dream about where they envision the agency going. Dreaming is the most critical point. It will set the pace for developing the unit's vision for functions, people involved, intended results, buy-in strategies, policies, and future implementation and assessment efforts.

Chapter 1 Sneak Peek - Training

- Creating a Vision of Your Team Blog:
  https://bit.ly/3F0Yp5R
- Building Legacy, Leadership, and Long-Term Success
  with Teams: https://bit.ly/3upwfwz
- Efficiency Strategies: https://bit.ly/3iirCzi

Many police agencies make the critical mistake of jumping into data, systems, technologies, and products first when establishing an analytical capacity rather than thinking with the end in mind. Analysts often spend massive amounts of resources and time implementing short-term thinking strategies, redundant activities, undervalued products, and thrown-together systems that evolve faster than the analyst supervisor can keep pace. They attend training after training to learn the newest tactics rather than pursuing intentional, proactive, and sustainable approaches.

With good intention, the supervisor/analyst immediately dives into responding to requests, building out statistical reports and bulletins that they *think* their agency needs. They often do this to get up and running quickly and to provide immediate value that promotes buy-in. However, in many cases, the agency does not fully grasp the value of the analytical function and, as a result, does not tap into its superpowers. Inevitably, the analyst succumbs to the excess of data entry and requests without the proper technical support required for success, and the agency fails to establish actual data-driven strategies. And the supervisor is putting out fires and trying to "convince" the agency that data-driven strategies work.

In this case, the agency started with the "what," and not the why, or intended outcomes, and thus has no compass pointing them in the right direction in terms of data-driven strategies.

Instead, to optimize one's analytical function, agencies must take the time first to understand where they are headed. A clear vision creates opportunities for the agency to discover possibilities. A clear vision creates focused intention. A clear vision is a compass, the roadmap that becomes the measure of success, and it provides macro and micro-objectives to reach. Creating a quality vision helps inspire the people who come on board with the team. It encapsulates the core values of an analytical function and helps people understand the actual capacity of a quality, data-driven operation.

Many authors, researchers, and transformational speakers start with *why*, including Steven Covey in his book "*The 7 Habits of Highly Effective People.*" Covey details the powerful lesson of thinking with the end in mind (Habit 2.) He describes the process of beginning with a vivid picture, image, or paradigm of what one seeks to achieve. The idea is that all things are created twice: once in the mind and once in reality. Upon completing that clear image of intention, these fundamental values guide all future actions and decisions relative to reaching that image.

Again, we see this concept with the famous Houston Oilers football player and acclaimed Broadway playwright and performer Bo Eason. In his book *There's No Plan B for Your A-Game. Be the Best in the World at What You Do,* Eason describes a process of making one's declaration of where they will be the best. He invites his readers to craft a drawing and mail him a letter dated twenty years into the future declaring what has been achieved and articulating obstacles overcome. He details that once a person defines where they are going, distractions and obstacles are simply determined to be steppingstones to getting there. These authors and many others have discovered the value of starting with a deep and clear vision.

To translate these concepts into policing, and specifically into building analytical capacity, agencies must start with the *why* and think with the end in mind. Go back to the earlier section and review the benefits of a true analytical legacy to begin to uncover why your agency desires analytical capacity. To provide opportunities for success for patrol and detectives? To be able to be confident about your numbers and produce them consistently? To identify timely patterns and trends and provide patrol with actionable direction? To provide detectives with investigative leads?

Creating a vision opens the agency up to possibilities. Supervisors and analytical staff become much more focused and intentional. Purposefully providing partners with the bigger picture helps them understand and value the analytical role more easily. Creating a vision inspires the team and raises hope and expectations. It is the compass that guides the entire team. It encapsulates core values. It is the roadmap to creating higher engagement and investment at all levels.

When performed correctly, creating a destination point provides the agency with a quality foundation, crystal-clear clarity, the right partners, and effective usage of long-term, sustainable analytics. The agency recruits and retains quality analysts, creates efficient and effective onboarding processes, instills buy-in and legacy from the beginning, and pivots with technologies rather than being driven by them. Agencies who start with vision create a commitment to excellence that guides all other activities and provides patrol, detectives, and all other partners with opportunities to succeed in their roles of service and safety.

Some agencies also produce a mission, a one-liner, and answer who you are, what you do, and why you do it. It does not change. A vision is different from a mission as it is vivid and describes long-term desired results (1-3 years into the future). A vision evolves and is revisited every six months to a year or so and adjusted based on the new or expanding vision of the unit.

Steps To Creating Your Agency Vision

Here are three steps to create a Vision Statement for your Unit.

Step 1: Decide who will play a role in the crafting of the vision. Start with some clarity around your thoughts using the questions below. Then bring in the partners (Chief, supervisors, analysts, etc.) to build out clarity around the vision.

Step 2: Dare to dream! Brainstorm. This stage involves imagining what the ideal unit looks like, who it serves, and how it serves. Dream big!

Step 3: Questions to answer:

- What do we want our unit to look like?
- Where are we going as a unit/agency?
- What do we want to achieve?

- What are our deliverables?
- What ultimate impact do we want to have?
- How will we interact with "clients"?
- What will our culture look like?

These steps will help you nail down a clear vision of where you and your unit are headed and will be the building blocks to continue your efforts. In addition to defining the vision, the analytical unit must also communicate that vision and create buy-in for the function.

> *Creating the vision is just the beginning!*

The book for supervisors creates clarity around the vision of your analytical unit. It explores more: the big picture of data-driven strategies, the roles and responsibilities of the analytical unit, policies, and procedures, how to recruit and retain quality analysts, collection tools, and data quality strategies, how to be results-focused and purpose-driven, turning data into actionable insight/predict and optimize outcomes, establishing influence and buy-in, developing efficiency strategies, building a legacy, leadership, and long-term success in crime analysis! There are tools and templates and examples – no starting from scratch! This comprehensive book and related program are a step-by-step, long-term approach to what you need to create trusted teams, be highly productive, and live a *happy* life - enjoying those people and activities in life that mean the world to you!

My next book about *Leadership* will be released in 2022. If you'd like to be notified when it's available, you can stay in touch here. https://excellenceinanalytics.com

CONCLUSION

> *"The only person you are destined to become is the person you decide to be."*
> — RALPH WALDO EMERSON

You now have seven action steps that will bring you closer to being an excellent analyst and leader of yourself! You discovered your Life By Design through the bubble chart. You understand that crafting your *why* establishes the direction towards which you will point your compass and the starting point for your professional and personal mastery. Now you can start building your professional development plan based on a couple of the skill sets we explored. Creating a plan with action steps and milestones will propel you closer to your vision and career goals. You can begin to think like a leader by shifting your mindset and creating effective habits and strategies in your life to increase your efficiency and effectiveness.

If you made it this far, you are now ready to take the next step – to be the one percent who excels. You want accelerated results. You want to discover and use even more tools to become a top law enforcement analyst while being incredibly successful and happy every step of the way! You want to take good care of yourself! You want to connect with your family and friends and live an authentic life of happiness and joy. You are ready to become the analyst who lives a life filled with fulfillment, confidence, value, and joy!

Here are three final tips for moving you forward in your future "bite out of life" endeavors.

- *DECIDE.* What do you want? I mean, what do you *really* want? Is this where you want to be, how you want to feel until you retire? You don't have to struggle with a lack of self-care, boundaries, and a stressful lifestyle. Become a better version of yourself! Simply *decide.*

- *LEADERSHIP OF SELF AS A PRIORITY.* Through my own experiences with overcoming work-induced adrenal fatigue, the "perfection" mask, and a scarcity mindset, I found *exactly* what it takes to be efficient, effective, connected, confident, happy, and excellent! You are the main character in your story. Build your life by design with self-love and *leadership of self* as a priority. You will not only operate at a higher level for others, but you will find more joy... and you deserve it! I sincerely believe that we can have it all - a remarkable career and a wonderful home life by design.

- *HIRE A QUALIFIED COACH.* Making the decision to prioritize you and implement what's required to do so isn't easy. And quite honestly, many analytical professionals in law enforcement have been spinning their wheels for years but it doesn't work. It doesn't get better. You can only see through your lenses! Hiring a coach is the best thing I did years ago, and I still have one today! Now I coach others. I love the clients we coach;

they get actual results! They build confidence, create better work-life harmony, excel in careers, and have *more joy*. It is possible! The answer is right in front of you. It's up to you to leap.

Together, we are shifting the law enforcement culture to intentionally choose and achieve an excellent career growth path alongside *leadership of self!* You are ready. You are equipped. You are empowered. Genius is yours. Now, *go get it!*

SPECIAL THANKS!

I am incredibly proud and honored to highlight the following analysts who have joined our *Rising GENIUSS* (RG) Family, committed to a better way and a life of career success and joy. Several of their stories were sprinkled throughout this book and are included below in alphabetical order to ignite a spark in you. I hope they inspire you as much as they inspire me and our team!

But first... a special thank you to our incredible team: Michelle Foster, our Technical Manager, who went through the program herself and completely transformed her life and now gives her gifts to grow our services; Caroline Collins, our Engagement Specialist, who shines her energy, talent, and creativity throughout all of her contributions to our community; Coach Rhea Gerstenkorn, one of our first program graduates and now an RG Coach whose attention to detail and progress accelerates so many other analysts; Coach Jen Coner, another graduate of both our RG and Leadership programs and now an RG Coach who fully embraces the mission to elevate others with impeccable elegance; and law enforcement analytical industry leader Annie Mitchell who co-leads our leadership programming and is my personal mentor. Without each of you none of this is possible. Our team makes my dreams a reality!

MORE SUCCESS HIGHLIGHTS!

It is important to me to include the following because I want them to know they are the true stories of success!

Alex L. is a law enforcement professional who started in our RG coaching programs in March 2020. Since then, she has participated in nine of our programs - learning, growing, and evolving! Recently, she was promoted to Police Planner, a coveted position responsible for performing complex, statistical, and analytical research work and supervising operations. Here is her story of resilience: https://bit.ly/3B0pi7G

Ali L. joined our first RG program several years ago, looking for more organization at work, more confidence, and more quality of life outside of work. With personalized coaching and determined action on her behalf, she built her skills and resume with our team and eventually landed a role at an agency and new state she has grown to love! We are proud of you, Ali! She shares, "This program has been AMAZING. I have been able to make changes to my weekly bulletin after only two weeks of participating in the program. Dawn provided concrete examples and templates to make the process easy. She has been a champion and supporter of analysts. I can't say enough about Dawn, her skills and knowledge, and her endless supply of positive energy!"

Alicia L. is an incredible analyst from Virginia who is excellent at solving crimes, identifying patterns, and making connections between cases. She came to RG to learn to create work-life harmony, build her confidence, and learn to keep her light shining. Now in round two of our RG Program, Alicia continues to grow, learn about her life by design, and develop successful work-life harmony habits. Recently she stepped out of her comfort zone and created a master database system that she shared at an NHTSA training to about one hundred analysts country-wide. Within a minute of the training's end, an inspired analyst called me directly and shared that she wanted to be like Alicia! Congrats Alicia, for continuously motivating others to be the best versions of themselves!

Andrew B. came to RG barely pulling his head above water from a challenging situation with his employer. He didn't feel valued at his agency and truly desired to be on a leadership path. He realized his foundation was missing and sought to create a more robust baseline to grow his career. He noted that his biggest challenge was believing in himself and finding his confidence. Through his work in RG and two cycles in RG Leadership so far, Andrew has grown exponentially! He is now on the path to a supervisory position, backed with an incredible leadership foundation. With the guidance of his coach, he also found hidden talents relative to building quality relationships and intelligence analysis that he now teaches to others in our group, including instruction at the IACA Conference! He found a closer connection to his spirituality, deepened his goal setting with his partner in his personal life, and even started a legacy business making toxin-free candles. Andrew is now more positive, more reflective, and more intentional – not just in his work life, but in his home life! We are so incredibly proud of you, Andrew! Hear Andrew's story here:

https://youtu.be/GpqAjqaa-1Q and https://bit.ly/3COqoUq

Angelica C. began as an analyst in a school police agency, struggling to find her footing and contribution to the agency. She deeply lacked confidence and was a self-proclaimed perfectionist. Throughout the RG Program and RG Leadership Program, Angelica found herself, released her fears, created healthy boundaries, and now has endless opportunities at her fingertips! She shares, "I learned so much about myself that I did not know. I gained an incredible work-life balance through my work with RG. I am a totally different person. I have so much confidence!"

Cristiane D. was seeking a crime analysis position to no avail. She felt lost and defeated and eventually joined our RG Program to build the foundation to get the job and life she wanted. Over several months she worked with one of our coaches to create clarity around her desired life by design. She soon landed a phenomenal career position as an analyst at a large Fortune 500 company. Cristiane focused on identifying a situation that would meet her personal goals, and she sharpened her skills in preparation for a successful interview process. Way to go, Cristiane!

Dianna F. participated in our RG program and then graduated into our RG Leaders Program. In just months, Dianna experienced tremendous progress. She established her open database connection to her RMS/CAD, developed a master crime analysis database, linked all her tables, and set up many queries and reports! This effort took months of determination and conversations to get the connection and sweat and tears building the back end! As a result, Diana now has easy and accurate access to her data and trusts her system! No more pulling data from a dumpy **RMS** export. No more manually typing data into Excel. No more not being able to answer in-depth questions about cases or people or patterns. Diana now automates reports, digs into her data with ease, and identifies patterns and trends. Diana put her CEO hat on and delivered what her agency needed in this capacity, leading her unit in other infrastructure growth areas. They are so lucky to have her! Congrats Diana!

Elizabeth's agency sent her to our **RG Program** to learn the ins and outs of what it takes to be a successful analyst. New to Crime Analysis, she quickly learned to build out her master database system, automate tons of reports, present outstanding Compstat events, and create analytical buy-in at her agency. She shares, "The resources EIA provided not only helped me to feel confident in the technical skills needed to create actionable products, but also encouraged me to clarify the purpose behind these products so that my time was used with more intention and resulted in greater impact. At the same time, this process prompted me to realize that my work and home life both reflect how well I am taking care of my well-being. Aligning my daily practices with my values (as a person, leader, wife, and coworker) has brought to fruition more confidence and connection than I thought impossible before starting this. Understanding the impact my leadership of self and in turn leadership of others has on my environment is a most empowering gift, and I am grateful my department offered me the opportunity to join EIA and discover that."

Erika B. is one of the most resilient analysts I know, and I am incredibly proud of her! She was gifted a spot in our RG Program by her agency and, during her time, saw incredible success. With our Compstat templates and technical assistance, she revamped a 100-paged Compstat process into a digestible, condensed, actionable report that assisted in strategy deployment and assessment. Erika also shifted her mindset and now considers herself a CEO of Crime Analysis (and her life!) She presents to groups, holds a leadership role with her regional analyst group, has dramatically reduced her stress and increased her confidence, and continues to take on challenges with pride, respect, and leadership of self. Erika shares, "My EIA coach and I have done one-on-one coaching. I initially thought it was just for work. I ended up uncovering confidence and resilience I never knew I had. My coach has a way of pushing me just outside my comfort zone for optimal growth and is always there for support. I couldn't have asked for a better coach and friend!"

Jane R. joined our RG Program to create better systems and more quality of life. Her work resulted in both! She shares, "I was feeling frustrated not really knowing how to move forward from where I was, and I feel like, in the past couple of months, I have been able to take great leaps towards where I ultimately would like to see my agency's crime analysis program go. This is stuff just three months ago I could only dream of doing. In fact, I don't think I could even have dreamed it! Thank you for all of your encouragement and all of the practical help, too!"

Jenna B. is one of my favorite analyst success stories! She was in our RG Program for three rounds, joining in to improve her self-confidence, her work-productivity confidence, and create better work-life harmony. It took her engine a little while to get heated, but once she got going, she was on fire! She went from not taking care of herself at all (she couldn't even look in the mirror) to taking excellent care of herself with monthly visits to the sauna, chiropractor, and acupuncturist. She reduced her chips and candy consumption at night by over 50%, developed systems at work that improved data quality and analytics, and found her friends and joy for life again. She finally realized she deserved her best life. Jenna also found her relationship with her son again, inspiring him to eat well, enjoy life, and build positive connections. Her life is completely different now and filled with excellence in her career and love for her home life. So proud of you, Jenna!

Jenn Z. is an RG member who recently saw an enormous triumph! She is a newer analyst to her agency (under two years,) trying to gain buy-in from her peers and the staff she serves. We all know this can be a big challenge! She was trying to figure out how to use the intelligence information that area agencies share with her that is important to her detectives. With the help of her coach, she developed an Access database to store this info and deliver actionable reports and investigative leads. She didn't stop there! Knowing how vital buy-in is, she developed a feedback loop with detectives to help determine what works best in terms of analysis and reporting, and they met to discuss progress! They brainstormed ways to make it better and support detectives and officers. And ... she recruited two detectives to be her guinea pigs and to start building stories! As a result, the team invited her to their lineups to present her intelligence insight weekly! Jenn recommends getting to know your officers and detectives personally - like working out together - and discussing non-work activities. She says that getting to know them better personally (and them her) is making their work conversations and growth so much easier! Congrats Jenn, for this and all your successes as a repeat RG member!

Jen C. became an RG Program client, RG Leadership client, and one of our incredible coaches in just a little over a year! Jen started with us as an analyst in Major Crimes and soon identified a significant gap in information available in unsolved murder cases. With her creativity, curiosity, ambition, and customized coaching and technical assistance, she digitally organized all the unsolved murder cases, representing over 140 victims. She and her agency now have detailed conversations around these investigations and tell the public sincerely that their cases are not forgotten. Jen's commitment to personal growth and her investment in herself moved her from reactive analyst to an innovative, creative, coveted leader at her agency and in industry. She continues to shed her light and commitment to excellence as one of our lead coaches, lifting others into their excellence. Listen to her success story here https://youtu.be/gq8F3yd91-w.

Jessica Y. is a long-time analyst supervisor searching for tools to build her analytical infrastructure within her agency. Quickly, she built analytical systems, developed her core leadership characteristics, and created a stronger work-life harmony. Go, Jessica! She shares, "This Leadership Incubator has in a sense given me the support I was looking for to work on creating the best version of myself. This is done with such honesty and thoughtfulness that it is impossible not to be moved to change. I am enormously grateful for the forces at work that led me to this leadership group, and I look forward to working and growing my leadership skills. I am finding myself being more intentional and long for meaningful change - inspiring me to join Facebook, just to have access to the Tribe, is nothing short of a small miracle."

Judith H., a Security Specialist, is an RG Program graduate and current RG Leadership member - join me in celebrating her success. She is responsible for coordinating multiple groups of industry experts who make recommendations to the TSA Administrator on surface transportation security. Since COVID, like most of us here, her team has had to transition to virtual connections - in her case, that's like herding sheep and calf and dragonflies all into one fenced-in area! She has successfully coordinated all the efforts of over 50 partners, despite being on lockdown! Somehow, she gathered all of their materials and strategies, ensured that they didn't overlap and that their efforts were united, and presented it all in unison during their July 30th meeting. We celebrate you and your determination and attention to detail! Congrats, Judith!

Justin R. came to us searching for any job in law enforcement analytics. With personalized coaching and skill development, Justin created clarity and an analytical foundation and soon landed a role as a drug intelligence analyst in another state. One month after moving his entire life to another state, he demonstrated leadership by seeking training opportunities for his coworkers and himself. He has also shared some valuable industry-specific training with his supervisor, of which his supervisor was unaware. Justin is establishing his skills foundation while also elevating others around him. Great job, Justin!

Kaitlyn W. took her future into her own hands, and I am so incredibly proud of her! She felt powerless, disheartened, and didn't know where to turn, searching for a career in Crime Analysis that never seemed to come. She took the leap into our RG Program, invested in her future (and as a waitress that took a huge financial commitment,) did the work, and found her dream job and her new life by design! So proud of you, Kaitlyn!

Kris K. came to our RG family seeking to improve her skills and contributions to her federal agency. We are so proud to share that Kris was selected as a Team Lead at her agency! Kris has been working hard to achieve this grand success - creating clarity and rocking out clear action steps alongside the guidance of her fabulous coach, Jennifer. Way to go, Kris!

Laura C. has seen incredible growth in just three months of being in our Wellness Coaching Program! Laura struggled with confidence and guilt for quite some time (heck, a ton of us do!) when she finally decided to create change in her life. Three months ago, she committed to round two of wellness coaching with our team - broken, disheartened, but hopeful and committed to change. She struggled with communicating with ease at work, connecting with her family, and working through the responsibilities of organizing her mother's estate. Week after week, she showed up gaining more and more clarity on her goals. She was vulnerable and committed to making change. There were uncomfortable tears and a manner of stretching she had not been able to do independently. Each session, she "showed up" with excellence. She executed success list after success list. I was so proud of her for her commitment to the process. After three months, Laura is finally getting above water. She has found absolute joy, pride, and love of herself. She has found her voice with her managers, has made deep connections to family and friends, and now takes excellent care of herself. Notably, she shared, "I never would have gotten to where I am without listening to you, even when I thought you were crazy. I did not think the program was going to fix me. But it worked! I showed up, did the work, and listened. I am taking better care of myself. I am proud of the work that I did with my mom's estate planning. My mom knew that she was loved and that it was okay to go and be with dad. Thanks for guiding me toward living my best life." She is a true success story. Her work, in our wellness program and her life, continues as she desires to reach even greater leadership of self. We are so proud of you, Laura!

Liz B. is a resilient policy researcher, activist, and yoga instructor who came to our RG Program with big goals and lots of life turmoil. She struggled with quality self-care, external factors beyond her control, and career choices at her fingertips. Liz did the work and found multiple levels of success throughout her experience. Liz shares, "I think one of the biggest things I took away from it was the 'be your own CEO' and also realizing that it's my job to discover what my boss and others want. It's a shift in mindset from being in a role and trying to please your superiors versus telling them what you think would work and how to engage with them to see what's working/what's not. I think it helps one be a little more creative and inspired, which is better than just being in a role."

Michelle F. joined our RG Program and, after working with her coach to align with her true desires, some she never even dreamt of, she gained the freedom to do the fun part of her job, gained financial independence, and built confidence like no one's business! She shares, "I set all these goals and smashed them one after the other, including buying a home! I give my agency a better work product because I am happier! The freedom that comes with knowing I have the confidence to get exactly what I want is truly an amazing feeling!" See her story here: https://youtu.be/QgIVLgDP5x0

Sgt. Nick just started diving into Crime Analysis this past year. He handles a ton of other responsibilities at his almost 200 officer agency. Yet, he takes the time to learn and grow! Through the RG Program, Sgt. Nick developed the infrastructure to build an analytical unit, including hiring an analyst and creating the job descriptions, policies, and procedures needed for a solid foundation. As an acting analyst until his hire, he learned how and what to analyze when a series came into his town. Sgt. Nick was able to flex his analytical muscles with a catalytic converter series we uncovered during one of our sessions. He designed a bulletin using the prediction models taught, and subsequently, his agency arrested the suspect. Congrats, Nick, for taking the lessons you learned and applying them! That takes courage, vulnerability, and belief! Rock on!

Nick R. was a multi-program participant, spending several rounds in RG and around in RG Leadership. Nick's private coaching centered around him sharing his analytical skills by building a business that served the technical needs of other analysts. Nick was able to develop training delivery systems, marketing strategies, and a business plan to help him achieve his dream! He released his fears and built his confidence, leading him into career success while connecting deeply with his family. (https://excellenceinanalytics.com/success-stories)

Patina C. is an analyst supervisor who is in round 2 in our RG Leadership Program. She has found tremendous success in building her leadership skills and her team and becoming more clear about the next steps in her career. She shares, "Being a part of the RG Leadership Incubator has improved my confidence in the job I am doing, brought more focus on work/life balance, and has provided amazing tools I can implement to be a better leader and team member. The ability to talk about issues and get ideas on how to be a better leader from other like-minded people in a safe, nonjudgmental environment has been one of the best parts of the program."

Rhea G. was an analyst at an agency undergoing extraordinary change with three different chiefs and many other moving leadership personnel. She lost her cheerleaders and found herself in an incredibly stressful work environment where many were jumping ship. She felt like she was on a ledge, ready to crash. As Kismet had it, one morning while scrolling LinkedIn, she saw an RG ad that read, "Do you want to find your genius?" and immediately leaped. Rhea regularly invested in her personal growth and knew she needed to dive into something big. Through the tears, the growth work, and the deep stares in the mirror, Rhea found herself again. She found her confidence, her path, her energy, her solution. Rhea smiled again. With her coach in her corner, she found a new job that better aligned with her skills and direction, released her imposter syndrome, and found a happier life by design. She graduated from our RG Leadership Program and is now one of our beloved coaches, guiding others into their authority, authenticity, and influence in their lives. We are incredibly proud of Rhea and the commitment she has as a leader in the industry! Listen to her story here: https://youtu.be/rbz8tlaJP8k.

Robyn K. joined our RG Program several years ago to find a better version of herself and connect to a career in analytics. She spent a week after work building her confidence, foundational skills, and critical thinking. She landed a job in her desired analytical field and made decisions based on her true desires. Way to go, Robyn!

Shannon K. started her career in the military, flourished in law enforcement as a civilian analyst, and now happily leads a team of software engineers as the Project Manager in a private sector company. She came to RG Leadership seeking support in transitioning her skills to the private sector, building her leadership skills, and finding herself after moving to another state and career path. Shannon continues to grow as an incredible leader in our programs, sharing and contributing with enthusiasm and strength. She has improved her boundaries with friends, nurtured her fun and healthy side, and shaped her leadership style with integrity and solidarity. She shares, "Come as you are and be supported by people who come from all walks of life. (RG Leadership) is a safe community to guide you through your personal and professional journey."

Here are even more amazing stories https://excellenceinanalytics.com/success-stories.

BONUS SECTION

After more than 23 years in service, I have heard every question, every challenge, every struggle a law enforcement analyst and supervisor face while building analytical capacity and influence as analytical specialists. Analysts in California, Massachusetts, Canada, and globally share common concerns. Ninety-nine percent of you will face similar issues at some point. Equipping yourself with action steps for success will bring you increased professionalism, confidence, and greater ease in your career. We work with analysts individually to dig deeper into their specific challenges and help with customized resolutions as each challenge arises. In conclusion, I want to leave you with a few more tools to address the top challenges and solutions you will encounter! Note that some of these have already been highlighted in previous chapters. Still, I want to have one place where it is convenient for you to find everything you require for success in your *Marketability, Professional Development, Fulfillment, & Joy!*

1. **What should I be doing as an analyst?**

   Your number one goal is *to provide actionable reporting so that your officers, command staff, and detectives can succeed.* That means that you are regularly identifying patterns and trends, identifying potential suspect leads, and contributing in an essential way to the operations of your agency. Visit your personal mission often! Whether you are new to analysis or a seasoned analyst who needs a boost, these five things are key activities that every analyst needs to do to be the CEO of their analytical role.

Check out this free download on 5 Things Analysts Must Do. https://bit.ly/3m8VDmf

2. How do I balance multiple and competing priorities?

- First, get a handle on all the products and activities you do. Use this Product Assessment Template https://bit.ly/39NvTpI to help. This tool allows analysts and supervisors to measure the productivity of activities and products, identify impact gaps, and provide ideas for filling those gaps.

- Second, check yourself! Are you wasting time? Are you performing repetitive tasks and not saving enough precious time for real analytics? Installing productivity habits is critical in creating simple practices and efficiencies that will bring you to the highest level of productivity. Analysts must focus on getting more quality work done in less time, accelerating you closer to your goals, and creating that work-life harmony you seek. Attend a free Peak Productivity Masterclass in our Tribe of Excellence https://bit.ly/3m8IUQG

- Facebook community to determine if you are focusing on the wrong things or view it online here:

- Third, review your job description in detail. Consider updating according to current priorities relative to the IMPACT that you and your agency desire. Our RG Program https://bit.ly/39OrJhv

- provides templates for new job descriptions that are actionable, purpose-focused, and attract the correct type of analyst.

1. *How do I deal with the data quality issues that make finding time for analysis impossible?*

Data quality must be a priority for an agency that genuinely desires to implement data-driven strategies. Although analysts are in the data regularly, they should *NOT* be considered the primary data quality agents of an agency's efforts. Instead, the analyst can identify data quality challenges that must be addressed on a systems level. The most long-term and time-efficient efforts involve creating systems of success at multiple levels within the agency. Click Data Quality Tips for Analysts https://bit.ly/3kRolZy for a free download on how to get started with implementing systemic data quality improvements.

2. *How do I create buy-in relative to the proper use of analytics at my agency?*

Creating a data-driven culture and buy-in within agencies must be a focused effort. First, analysts must be deliberate, purposeful, and positioned as an authority to gain influence and respect as an integral component of the agency's strategic operations. Second, creating buy-in and influence must be intentional and persistent agency-wide and include building and nurturing internal relationships. Strategies that agencies can implement today will lead to more significant influence and buy-in, flowing feedback loops, and a more robust and fully integrated data-driven function. In the end, buy-in and influence strengthen the utility of the agency's desired analytical results and provide opportunities for officers to succeed. Check out this free audio and download Creating Buy-In and Influence https://bit.ly/3CYbBqo to learn ten tips to create influence at your agency. In addition, relationship-building should be intertwined into the daily schedule of an analyst! Here are some free tools to get you started:

- Law enforcement analysts and supervisors can use this tool to build high-quality relationships in your career and your personal life! Building Relationships Free Download https://bit.ly/2YapgvE
- Building Strong Relationships Blog https://bit.ly/3F2W6iF
- A step-by-step on building quality relationships in policing.
- Our YouTube Playlist https://bit.ly/3kTjhns building quality relationships.

3. I am really struggling with work-life harmony. Where do I begin?

First, *decide.* Decide what you want your life to look like. Use this free Life by Design https://dawnreeby.podia.com/free-life-by-design-download download to gain clarity on your purpose and desired lifestyle. This is the roadmap to becoming a purpose-driven analytical professional who delivers impact while maintaining your well-being. Second, try these Analyst Mantras https://dawnreeby.podia.com/analyst-mantras on for size and see how they create a more quality day.

4. How do I deal with not having a clear direction from management regarding vision, assignments, and similar?

Start with your clear vision! Creating a vision opens the agency up to possibilities. Supervisors and analytical staff become much more focused and intentional. Purposefully providing partners with the bigger picture helps them understand and value the analytical role more easily. Creating a vision inspires the team and raises hope and expectations. It is the compass that guides the entire team. It encapsulates core values. It is the roadmap to creating higher engagement and investment at all levels. Click here on our blog for steps to creating your vision: https://bit.ly/3kPbtmO.

5. How do I deal with limited resources for equipment, training, etc.?

The fact is, you can deliver the end product – actionable reporting so that you officers and detectives can succeed – on a napkin! You don't need fancy equipment. Yes, it makes life a lot easier. But it isn't necessary for you to be of value. For a basic, quality function, I recommend two to three monitors, a basic Microsoft package with Word, Excel, Access, PowerPoint, and Publisher. You may also consider a mapping software such as ArcPro (your City may have a GIS tool that you can tap into at little to no extra cost). If nothing else, BatchGeo is a simple, free tool that gives you the ability to perform basic mapping.

In addition, there are a ton of free and low-cost resources available, including:

- DDACTS IADLEST training home page: https://bit.ly/3m4wysK
- NHTSA Automation Series including Analyst Library: https://bit.ly/3kOt4v4
- IADLEST Multi-part Analytical Training Series: https://bit.ly/2XZzvCu

- BJA Crime Analysis Webinars (for Commanders AND Analysts): https://www.iadlest.org/training/crime-analysis-webinar
- DDACTS Operational Guidelines: https://www.iadlest.org/training/ddacts/documents
- IACA has a ton of great training found here https://iaca.net/
- ILET has a ton of great training found here https://ilet.network/
- Lots of free training on our YouTube Excellence in Analytics https://www.youtube.com/channel/UCfkXoJCB2mNhVyslMswWBUA
- Our Tribe of Excellence Facebook https://www.facebook.com/groups/171925267401670 community has weekly free live training and numerous training announcements.
- More free training found here: https://excellenceinanalytics.com/blog/f/quality-resources-for-law-enforcement-analysts

6. *How do I improve my skills or know what skills to improve?*

A professional development roadmap based on the desired results relative to the vision, skills, talents, and passions of the analyst must be established, prioritized, and visited regularly. The roadmap should include relative training, quality networking, instructional efforts, building buy-in, leadership development, and other results-focused growth opportunities. Essentially, agencies must think with the end in mind when developing a roadmap to fill gaps, encourage learning, and promote ownership and growth. Our <u>RG Program</u> <u>https://dawnreeby.podia.com/risinggeniussprogram</u> thoroughly assesses the skills of any analyst (crime, intelligence, etc.) and designs a progressive and customized plan with each client. You can also get started with this free <u>Power Planning Matrix</u> <u>https://dawnreeby.podia.com/ffd38b02-d6f7-45b2-a86c-29b6fd798b96</u> to create a structure to your goals in each of the core focus areas key to industry success and work-life harmony.

Government mindset - It's important to point out that many analysts live in this government mindset, meaning they only attend training and professional development opportunities that their departments pay for and tell them to attend. I believe that we must take hold of our *own* professional development. We must get out of the mindset that the government will tell us what to be trained on. We must adopt a continuously growing and learning mentality, regardless of who foots the bill. Your development must be a priority for you! And we must consider developing more than just our hard skills. This is a <u>great video</u> <u>https://www.youtube.com/watch?-v=gq8F3yd91-w</u> on taking charge of your career!

7. *How do I set clear goals? I never seem to have time to achieve the big stuff!*

Our <u>Goal Crafting and Achieving</u> <u>https://bit.ly/3iivJeI</u> free download will help you create a plan for the next chapter of your life, creating the *right* goals and developing intentional *action steps* to reach them!

8. **How do I get recognized as an analyst when I contribute to the successes at the agency? How do I build my confidence?**

Building a portfolio of work products (that is appropriately redacted) accomplishes a few things. First, it's a quick reference source for you to recall how much you have contributed to your agency's mission. Next, it's a tangible visual for your supervisors to understand your role, skills, and talents. Finally, regular review of your portfolio will guide you quickly towards the next milestone you want to see reflected in your portfolio so you can choose relevant training. We reviewed all the steps for you to build a portfolio in Module 5, on pages 103-104.

ABOUT THE AUTHOR

Dawn Reeby is the CEO of Excellence in Analytics (EIA) and is an energetic subject matter expert, keynote speaker, author, trainer, and coach with success in leadership training and data-driven operations development. Her mission is to ignite the desire for excellence in professional and personal life and empower the pursuit of that excellence. Dawn is the 2021 recipient of the International Association of Crime Analysts (IACA) Bryan Hill Award. This award recognizes an individual who embodies "Spirit of Service" in the Crime Analysts industry. She is a highly sought-after strategist and high-performance coach known for creating skilled, balanced, and highly productive leaders and professionals. Dawn also partners with various federal, state, and local agencies as a law enforcement strategy specialist and subject matter expert, designing and delivering nationally certified and international courses, webinars, day-and-week-long workshops, and keynote speeches. She is the host of multiple platforms that help social sector professionals skyrocket their results, multiply their productivity, and connect with other high-level, service-based thinkers from around the world! She is also a certified Holistic Health Coach from the Institute of Integrative Nutrition (December 2021) and works to improve global health and holistic life happiness.

Dawn and her team at EIA work with law enforcement professionals to help them be excellent in their work commitments *in unison* with a home life that they love! EIA coaches are phenomenal at helping public sector professionals align proactive career strategies with wellness priorities so that these heroes can perform service with excellence while discovering their path to happiness. They shift from *reactive* to *proactive* strategies and, as a result, become better able to fulfill their work mission with precision and ease *and* finally live a life of happiness, fulfillment, and joy.

Company Website: https://excellenceinanalytics.com/
Programs: https://dawnreeby.podia.com/
LinkedIn: https://www.linkedin.com/in/dawn-reeby-%F0%9F%92%AB-high-performance-coach-and-wellness-strategist-3b24439b/
Instagram: @excellenceinanalytics
Blog: https://excellenceinanalytics.com/blog
YouTube:
https://www.youtube.com/channel/UCfkXoJCB2mNhVyslMswWBUA
Facebook: TRIBE OF EXCELLENCE is a Facebook community of service-based and emergency response professionals who work to create the social impact they desire while living their best lives!
https://www.facebook.com/groups/171925267401670

Hi. I'm Dawn Reeby, author of *Bigger Than Data*.
I want you to achieve a work-life harmony that sings!

<u>CLICK HERE</u> to grab a day/time on my calendar and let's
build out a plan to achieve your goals.

https://calendly.com/dawn_reeby/30-minute?month=2021-09

Can't wait to connect :)

– Dawn

WE HAVE A BIG FAVOR TO ASK - WILL YOU HELP US?

Thank You For Reading *Bigger Than Data!*

I really appreciate your feedback, and I love hearing your ideas about the book and how you relate to these stories - and how you are taking action! The team at Excellence in Analytics (EIA) wants to know that the content we deliver and the training we provide are making a difference!

Please go to Amazon today and share your thoughts about the book. We appreciate your time and feedback *ginormously*! 🖤

Thanks again!

— Dawn Reeby

Made in USA - Kendallville, IN
85165_9781938953200
11.11.2021 0351